Routledge Revivals

The Politics of Preferences

The Politics of Preferences (1975) examines the development of European Community trade policy between 1963 and 1973 and its impact on developing countries. It also looks at the strategy and tactics pursued by developing countries during the same period in an attempt to get a better deal for their exports to the Community and other developed countries. It examines bargaining – and power and weakness – and the way in which the Community takes – or fails to take – decisions.

The Politics of Preferences

EEC Policy Making and the Generalised System of Preferences

Peter Tulloch

Routledge Revivals
Routledge
Taylor & Francis Group

First published in 1975
by Croom Helm Ltd

This edition first published in 2026 by Routledge
4 Park Square, Milton Park, Abingdon, Oxon, OX14 4RN

and by Routledge
605 Third Avenue, New York, NY 10017

Routledge is an imprint of the Taylor & Francis Group, an informa business

Publisher's Note
The publisher has gone to great lengths to ensure the quality of this reprint but points out that some imperfections in the original copies may be apparent.

Disclaimer
The publisher has made every effort to trace copyright holders and welcomes correspondence from those they have been unable to contact.

A Library of Congress record exists under LCCN: 75308202

ISBN: 978-1-041-27935-8 (hbk)
ISBN: 978-1-003-75697-2 (ebk)
ISBN: 978-1-041-27940-2 (pbk)

Book DOI 10.4324/9781003756972

The Politics of Preferences

EEC policy making and the generalised system of preferences

PETER TULLOCH

CROOM HELM LONDON

in association with

THE OVERSEAS DEVELOPMENT INSTITUTE

First published 1975

Croom Helm Ltd
2-10 St. Johns Road, London SW11

ISBN: 0–85664–275–4

Set by Red Lion Setters, Holborn, London
Printed and bound in Great Britain by
Redwood Burn Limited, Trowbridge & Esher

CONTENTS

ACKNOWLEDGEMENTS

Most of the research for this book was undertaken during 1973. A large number of people helped in various ways in its creation. Particular thanks are due to members of the consultative committee convened by ODI, who read and commented on the drafts, both individually and collectively; to the officials of the Community, its member states, GATT, OECD and UNCTAD, who willingly consented to be interviewed and provided every possible assistance; and to Max Kohnstamm, Diarmid McLaughlin and Henri Perroy of the European Community Institute for University Studies, who provided needed working space in Brussels and helped greatly through their contacts with and intimate working knowledge of the Community. Any errors of fact which remain in the book are my own responsibility, as are the opinions expressed.

Finance for the book was provided by the Social Science Research Council, the Nuffield Foundation and the Overseas Development Administration. To them, too, grateful acknowledgements are due.

1. INTRODUCTION

This book is about the development of European Community trade policy between 1963 and 1973 and how developing countries were affected by it. It is also about the strategy, and to a lesser extent the tactics, pursued by developing countries during the same period in an attempt to get a better deal for their exports to the Community and other developed countries. It is about bargaining, and about power and weakness: the relative weakness of developing countries in the face of rich country governments' obstinacy, and the relative weakness (at least during the period under discussion) of pressure within the Community towards greater freedom of access for ldcs. And it is about the way the Community takes – or fails to take – decisions.

It is easy, with hindsight, to point to mistakes in bargaining tactics and strategy, and to say what should have been done instead of what was. But the evidence presented here suggests that developing countries' attempts to pursue a combined, consolidated strategy in trade discussions with the developed world may have been misdirected, and that the strength of resistance by politicians and lobbies in developed countries may have been underestimated. It also shows just how long it can take to make relatively small changes in policies at the international level where powerful partners' essential interests (as they perceive them) are likely to be jeopardised by change.

The main thrust of the ldcs' efforts internationally in the decade covered by the book was to persuade developed countries to grant their exports of manufactured and processed goods better terms: and not just better terms than existed before, but preferential terms – lower levels of import duty, and fewer quota restrictions and non-tariff barriers, than are imposed on imports from other developed countries. The developing countries pressed for concessions to set right basic inequalities of trade relations, and the principles on which their pressure was based were, first, that any reductions in tariffs or other trade barriers on products imported from ldcs should not have to be matched by reciprocal treatment of Western exports by the ldcs; second that preferential access should be truly preferential, i.e. discriminate in favour of ldcs. These principles were expressed in a general demand by ldcs for a Generalised System of Preferences (GSP).

As eventually introduced in the early 1970s, the GSP comprises 12 separate schemes operated by developed Western and State-trading countries or trading groups.[1] Under most of these schemes, most manufactured goods exported by developing countries may be imported duty-free into the developed countries which operate GSP schemes, if they meet certain quite stringent rules of origin. Some processed agricultural goods may also enter either duty-free or at tariff rates lower than the 'most favoured nation' level.

The Community was the first developed area to introduce a GSP scheme. Its scheme came into operation in July 1971 and was renewed at the beginning of 1972 and 1973. In January 1974, Britain and Denmark, which had introduced their own GSP schemes in January 1972, merged them with the GSP of the 'Six' to form a single, unified scheme for the enlarged Community.[2] Some improvements in commodity coverage were made and other changes have been proposed for 1975.

In the early 1960s, when first mooted, the type of non-reciprocal discriminatory treatment in favour of ldcs as a group implied by the GSP was something completely new for most developed countries. For the EEC this was certainly true. The Community's trade policies – and some would argue its identity – are based on the existence of a customs union inside a single, generally applicable common external tariff. At the time, the only exceptions to this general rule were the association agreements with Greece (1961) and Turkey (1963) individually and the association with French, Belgian and Italian colonies in Africa which was to become the Yaoundé Conventions of 1964 and 1969. None of these agreements, moreover, was based on non-reciprocity. The Greek association, aimed at eventual Community membership,[3] bound Greece to abolishing tariffs against EEC exports over twelve years (twenty-two for infant industries) in return for duty-free entry to the Community market by 1970 at the latest (1968 in practice) for Greek manufactures and special treatment for agricultural exports. The association agreement with Turkey initially extended preferential reductions in EEC duties, within tariff quotas, to imports of tobacco, raisins, nuts and figs; in 1970 a new protocol foresaw the establishment of a customs union between the EEC and Turkey in twenty-two years.[4] Similarly, the preferential access to EEC markets given to Yaoundé Associates was, in principle at least, matched by preferential entry for Community exports to the African markets under the 'free trade area' provisions of the Yaoundé Convention.

Again, for the Community as for other developed countries, the GSP was the only area of trade policy to consider ldcs as a distinct and discrete group to be treated in common. It is still the only area of Community policies towards developing countries, apart from food aid, not based on a specific regional or bilateral agreement. Since its introduction, however, the dichotomy between the Community's commitment to association and wider views of its policy aims and responsibilities has been more clearly defined; and the Commission's own attitude to the distinction between associable and non-associable countries has changed, as a result both of the negotiations during 1973-74 for a new, enlarged association and of the effects on ldcs of the 1974 oil, food and fertiliser crisis.

The GSP system has not fulfilled developing countries' expectations. The United States government has not yet introduced a GSP scheme, although it has submitted various proposals over time; and the possibility of its doing so is still in some doubt. It has taken a very long time for the developed countries to negotiate among themselves on the subject – the idea of the GSP was first mooted in 1962/63; and even by the time the GSP first came into force, changing events and pressures had reduced its immediate effectiveness. More importantly, however, the GSP schemes which have been introduced are much more limited than most developing countries had hoped, and it is possible that a new round of trade liberalisation negotiations in GATT, in which most developing countries are to take part,[6] will cut back the preferential benefits gained under the GSP by reducing the most-favoured nation (mfn) tariff rates.

The first aim of this study is to examine the process of political decision making which led up to the introduction of the Community's GSP in 1971. It evaluates the bargain which was struck within the Community and the weight which particular member states among the Six,[7] and the EEC Commission, brought to bear in this bargain. It reviews the main supranational, national and sectoral interests at work within the Community and the pressures exerted on it from outside, and attempts to show how conflicts of interests were resolved and how far, if at all, dominant pressures created a consistent bias in any one direction. And it shows the Community at work, as a body, negotiating with other major trading countries in a specific field of external policy agreed to be a joint Community responsibility. Broadly, this is covered in Chapters 4 to 7.

But the aims of the study are not purely historical: the GSP is still a live issue, and one major element in the present relations of the enlarged Community with developing countries. There are three main strands involved here; first, the negotiations in progress between the Community, its twenty-two original African Associates,[8] Ethiopia, Liberia, the Sudan, and the African, Caribbean and Pacific Commonwealth countries offered association with the EEC under Protocol 22 of the Treaty of Accession signed by the U.K., Denmark and Ireland.[9] The second factor is the part played by the GSP in the development of a wider policy towards developing countries, including the Commonwealth Asian countries covered by a Joint Declaration of Intent (JDI) annexed to the Treaty of Accession.[10] The third element is the role of the GSP in the 1974-75 round of GATT negotiations whose aims, as defined by an initial ministerial declaration made in Tokyo in September 1973,[11] are to reduce both tariff and non-tariff barriers to trade. In this context, the relevance of the GSP (which relates only to tariffs) in a trading world where non-tariff obstacles to trade, including 'voluntary' export limitation schemes, are still growing must be called into question.

The influence of African Associates on past Community policy is touched on in Chapter 6, in examining the historical development of the GSP, and discussed more fully in Chapter 7. There can be little doubt that the interest of Associates was one of the main factors which restricted the Community scheme's product coverage, and that the Community scheme might have been more broadly based if the USA in particular had been prepared to introduce a GSP which gave tariff preferences to EEC Associates. The attitudes of new Associates to the tariff preferences from which they benefit in Community markets will, similarly, condition the attitude of the enlarged Community to the future improvement of the GSP.

Chapters 8, 9 and 10, in turn, discuss the value of the GSP to developing countries, and the interests which ldcs at large are likely to have in its maintenance and improvement, on the one hand, or in moving away from preferential, discriminatory terms of access to developed countries' markets to simple tariff-free treatment on a par with domestic producers and the most favoured alternative source of imports.

The process of EEC enlargement and the creation of a widely based European free-trade area with the rump of EFTA have led to increased discrimination against non-associated ldcs. Table 1.1 sets out the hierarchy of trade relations surrounding the enlarged Community. Equality of treatment with the most favoured members of this hierarchy might be equally well achieved by non-preferential reductions in trade barriers as by the extension of 'preferences', however widely 'generalised'.

Demands for non-reciprocity have not, so far, achieved outstanding success in liberalising access to developed country markets for ldcs. One major reason has simply been the unattractiveness, in a protectionist world, of making one-sided concessions. How can ldcs now approach this problem? Those with needed natural mineral and agricultural resources may be able to exert pressure on developed countries to liberalise access for their processed and manufactured goods, either within bilaterally negotiated deals or on a global basis. Others are in a much more difficult situation, unless access for their products can be gained on the coat-tails of resource-rich ldcs.

But it is often maintained that – since trade liberalisation is

TABLE 1.1

THE HIERARCHY OF EEC TRADING RELATIONS

Group of Countries	
1. Enlarged EEC (9)	Free trade in *all goods* by 1977.
2. EFTA partners	Free trade in *manufacturers* by 1977
3. Existing Yaoundé associates (18)	Duty free entry to EEC market for all goods except those governed by Common Agricultural Policy, in return for limited 'reverse preferences'.
4. New 'Commonwealth associables' (20-23)	Possibility of same trading terms as Yaoundé associates; *probably* formal abolition of reverse preference requirement in new Association Convention.
5. Mediterranean* countries	Varying terms; Greece, Turkey, Malta, Tunisia, Morocco have differing 'associate' status. Generally duty-free entry with some limited concessions on CAP products.
6. Other LDCs	Limited duty-free access for manufactures under GSP. 20% tariff cuts for small number of processed agricultural products. No concessions on CAP products.
7. Other developed* countries	'Most-favoured nation' access.

* Some countries have negotiated product by product agreements with the EEC which give a few goods free access.

considered to have benefits for both exporting and importing countries in terms of economic efficiency – several developing countries could benefit from reducing their own excessively high levels of domestic protection.[12] Used as a bargaining counter in overall trade negotiations in GATT, this might produce more constructive results in getting trade barriers reduced on goods which developing countries are interested in exporting, than a purely one-sided demand for 'concessions' from developed country trade partners. The final aim of the study, then, is to review the bargaining possibilities which may exist for developing countries in dealing with the developed world in general and the European Community in particular: and to suggest (if at all) how the rather limited liberalisation of access to ldc exports achieved in the GSP might be carried further by ldc participation in the GATT negotiations.

NOTES

1. These are: EEC, Norway, Sweden, Finland, Austria, Switzerland, Japan, New Zealand; Bulgaria, Czechoslovakia, Hungary; and Australia (whose scheme, in action since 1966, is not, strictly speaking, part of the GSP network, but has some similar features).
2. This had been agreed in the Treaties of Accession: see Cmnd. 4815, Protocol 23 (HMSO, January 1973).
3. The association with Greece has been largely frozen since the military of 1967. The restoration of democracy in 1974 opened the way to its resumption.
4. For a detailed analysis of the agreement with Greece and notes on the Turkish association, see Stanley Henig, *External Relations of the European Community,* Chatham House/PEP, 1971.
5. October 1974.
6. Inaugurated in September 1973.
7. Belgium, France, West Germany, Italy, Luxembourg and the Netherlands.
8. The countries concerned are Burundi, Cameroon, Central African Republic, Chad, Congo (Brazzaville), Dahomey, Gabon, Ivory Coast, Malagasy Republic, Mali, Mauritania, Mauritius, Niger, Rwanda, Senegal, Somalia, Togo, Upper Volta and Zaire (Yaoundé Convention), Kenya, Tanzania, Uganda (Arusha Convention).
9. The countries concerned are Bermuda, Belize, the British Virgin Islands, Brunei, the Ceylon Islands, the Falklands, the Gilbert and Ellice Is., Montserrat, New Hebrides, Pitcairn Is., St. Helena, the Seychelles, Turks & Caicos Is., and the West Indies Associated States (dependencies); the Bahamas, Barbados, Botswana, Fiji, the Gambia, Ghana, Guyana, Jamaica, Lesotho, Malawi, Nigeria, Sierra Leone, Swaziland, Trinidad, Tonga, W. Samoa and Zambia (independent states).
10. India, Pakistan, Bangladesh, Malaysia, Sri Lanka and Singapore.
11. GATT Press Release 1134, 14 September 1973.
12. Professor Bela Balassa has put this argument particularly strongly in *The Structure of Protection in Developing Counties,* John Hopkins/IBRD, 1971.

2. THE COMMUNITY'S PREFERENCE SCHEME

The 1971 GSP

The EEC's scheme, introduced in July 1971, was originally set out in nine Regulations published in the Community's *Official Journal* on 28 June 1971. Rules of origin for the scheme were set out in further regulations published on 30 June and 11 October 1971. Although in principle the scheme was intended to run for ten years, formal agreement to its renewal has had to be given each calendar year by the Council of Ministers. This has not, so far, constituted any threat to the continuation of the scheme. Minor alterations to the operation of the scheme were made in the new regulations introduced in 1972 and 1973, and a major review undertaken in 1973 led to important changes of detail being made on its enlargement in 1974 to cover the Community of Nine. But the basic principles have remained the same throughout.

In the 1971-73 scheme, the Community granted preferential duty-free treatment, within limits, to all industrial products in BTN[1] chapters 25-99 covered by its scheme. Since, in the Community's view, the scheme was intended to cover only manufactures and semi-manufactures, all primary products in these BTN chapters, and all metals up to the ingot stage of processing, were excluded.[2] Preferences on jute and coir products were held back pending the conclusion of 'voluntary' export limitation agreements with the main producers (India and Bangladesh). Duty-free access on cotton goods extended only to countries which had signed similar 'voluntary' agreements under the GATT Long Term Arrangement on Cotton Textiles or which were prepared to enter into comparable agreements with the Community.[3] On other textiles, clothing and footwear, only independent states might benefit: a proviso made principally with the aim of excluding Hong Kong.

A system of ceilings on the total amount of preferential imports from all beneficiaries was fundamental to the scheme's treatment of manufactures. In principle, a ceiling level was set to duty-free imports of any manufactured good included. In practice, however, a distinction was made between sensitive, semi-sensitive and non-sensitive products, depending on the extent to which goods competed with Community domestic manufactures. Tariff quotas, establishing the total duty-free amount, were applied rigidly to imports of 'sensitive' manufactures; but for products in the less sensitive groups they were held in reserve, although they were more likely to be enforced on semi-sensitive products (the lists of which were not published) than on others. They consisted of two parts: a 'basic amount' (cif value[4] of imports into the Six in 1968 from beneficiaries) and a variable 'supplementary amount' (5 percent of the cif value of imports from all other countries outside the Community, based on 1968 for 1971, 1969 for 1972 and 1970 for 1973).[5] They were subdivided into 'buffer quotas' *(butoirs)* defining the amount of goods which could be imported duty-free from any one developing country; these were generally set at 30 percent of the overall tariff quota for 'sensitive' products. Fixed proportions of tariff quotas were also allocated to each member state.[6]

Processed agricultural goods in BTN chapters 1-24 were treated differently from manufactures. Only a small number of products was included in the system; and goods on which EEC protection was provided *only* by Common Agricultural Policy variable levies, as distinct from import duties, were excluded. UNCTAD estimated that the maximum value of imports of processed agricultural goods imported into the EEC in 1970, on which the type of scheme operating in 1972 would have extended tariff prefererences had it been in operation at the time, would have been $44m. or 1.8 percent of the Six's dutiable imports of goods in BTN chapters 1-24.[7] The margin of preference given on processed agricultural goods was very small, amounting to 20 percent of the total import duty as a rule (or, at the most, four or five percentage points).

To gain preferential entry under the scheme all products imported from developing countries were required to comply with rules of origin agreed in UNCTAD and laid down in 1971. Products 'originating in' a beneficiary country or dependency were generally required either to be wholly produced there, or to have undergone sufficient processing in the country of origin to be classified under a different tariff heading from that of any of the parts or materials used in manufacture. However, the rules contained a long, detailed list of provisos setting out minimum local value added criteria or defining particular types of product used in the manufacturing process which must also be locally produced.[8] Developing countries hoping to benefit from the GSP also had to furnish the Community customs authorities with specimen prints of the official Customs stamps used for verifying origin certificates. By August 1974, 68 independent developing countries and 13 dependencies had done so. But there is little doubt that these rules inhibited the rapid implementation of GSP for many countries.[9]

TABLE 2.1

'NEW PRODUCTS' ADDED TO EEC GSP LIST OF PROCESSED AGRICULTURAL GOODS IN 1974

BTN HEADING		DESCRIPTION	DUTIES CHARGED mfn	GSP
0201 AIII	b)	'Other' pigmeat	5%	Free
0303 AIV	a)	Prawns, fresh, chilled, frozen	12%	8%
0503 B		'Other' horsehair and waste	1%	Free
0515 AI		Dried shellfish, not for food	5%	Free
0704 ex B		Horseradish	16%	10%
0801 ex E		Desiccated coconut	4%	Free
0805 D		Pistachios	2%)	
E		Pecans	4%)	Free
F		Cola nuts	3%)	
ex G		Other nuts excl. hazelhuts	4%)	
0810 ex B		Quinces, frozen	20%	16%
0811 ex D		Quinces, provisionally preserved	11%	8%
0812 E		Dried pawpaws	4%	Free
0902 A		Packaged tea under 3 kg	5%	Free
0909 A III	b) 2	Fennel, cumin, caraway, juniper seed	5%	Free
1208 E L		Locust bean seeds, whole	2%	Free
C		Apricot, peach, plum stones	4%	Free
1302		Conifer resins	0.5%	Free
1401A II		Osier, 'other'	2%	Free
1507 B		Chinawood & oiticica oils	3%	1%
D I a) ex 3		Coconut oil for industrial use.	5%	2.5%
1510 C		Other fatty acids	4.5%	Free
1512 A		Solidified oils and fats under 1 kg.	20%	16%
B		Solidified oils and fats over 1 kg.	17%	12%
1517 B I		Oil foots and dregs: soapstocks	5%	Free
II		Other fatty residues	2%	Free
1604 ex F, ex G		Canned bonito, mackerel, hake & pilchards	25%	20%
1704		'Other' sugar confectionery	13%+	10%+
1804		Cocoa butter, fat or oil	12%	8%[1]
ex 2006		Canned pineapple chunks	23%	12%[2]
2102 ex A		Soluble coffee	18%	9%[3]
2201 A		Spa and aerated waters	4%	Free
2203		Beer	24%	19%
2301 B		Fish meal	2%	Free
2306 B		'Other' vegetable-based animal feeds	2%	Free
2404 D		Chewing tobacco, snuff	65%	52%
E		Other, including sheet & strip tobacco	26%	19%

NOTES

1. Tariff quota of 21,600 tonnes
2. Tariff quota of 20,000 tonnes overall. Plus levy on sugar.
3. Tariff quota of 18,750 tonnes.

The enlarged scheme for 1974 and 1975

The form of the GSP scheme applied by the Nine from 1 January 1974[10] was very much the same as the Six's earlier scheme. The provisions for manufactures fell into three groups: industrial products in general, cotton and competing textiles previously covered by the GATT Long Term Arrangement[11] and other textile products and footwear. Once again, each of these groups was divided into list of 'sensitive', 'non-sensitive' and 'semi-sensitive' (unpublished) products.

The main change from 1973 was to bring forward the base year for the calculation of tariff quotas and ceilings on products other than textiles from 1968 to 1971. The EEC Commission estimated that this measure would add around 40 percent to the overall value of tariff quotas on sensitive products which would have resulted from the application in 1973, by the Nine, of the scheme then in force for the Six.[12] The 'general' list of sensitive products was slightly reduced: twelve products previously treated as sensitive[13] were moved to the 'semi-sensitive' category, while three new products[14] were added to the sensitive list. Tariff quotas were subdivided, as before, first by *butoirs* set at 50 percent of the total for 'non-sensitive' and at 30 percent or 20 percent for 'sensitive' products, and second by the allocation of importing country quotas among each member state.[15] For textiles, the overall ceilings for sensitive and non-sensitive products together were re-calculated to allow double the value of goods to gain duty-free entry into the Nine; buffer quotas operated in the same way as for other manufactures, but the key under which importing country quotas were determined was changed slightly to allow Denmark, as a country more reliant on textile imports than any other of the Nine, to take 7 percent rather than 5 percent of the total.

The provisions agreed for processed agricultural goods – which were the most troublesome part of the intra-Community GSP negotiations of 1973 – were, from the point of view of the Six, a considerable expansion of those contained in the original scheme which had remained completely unchanged since 1971. But they still fell well short of the duty-free access granted by the original British and Danish schemes, and even further short of what most developing countries would probably have wanted. The main improvements in this field were a doubling of the margin of preference, from 20 to 40 percent of the mfn duty rate in most cases, and the addition of a number of extra products to the list, of which the most significant were packaged tea, coconut oil, cocoa butter[16], canned pineapples and instant coffee.[17]

While the new measures for processed agricultural goods represented a fairly large improvement in trading terms as far as the original Six were concerned, the tariffs which would be imposed would still have meant high new duty impositions in the British market for goods from non-associable Commonwealth developing countries (principally India, Bangladesh, Sri Lanka and Malaysia), and would also have increased duties on a number of goods which Britain, in particular, had been importing duty-free in its previous GSP scheme. Transitional arrangements, settled after long negotiations, allowed the three new members to charge only 20 percent or 40 percent (depending on the product) of the difference between their lowest rates of duty and the Community GSP rates, where their own lowest rates were below the GSP levels. For Britain this meant that many Commonwealth ldc imports bore only small levels of new duty in 1974.

New tariff quotas, at reduced rates of duty, were opened for cocoa butter (21,600 tonnes at 8 percent, rather than 12 percent), instant coffee (18,750 tonnes at 9 percent, rather than 18 percent) and canned pineapple chunks and pulp (20,000 tonnes at 12 percent rather than up to 24 percent under the CET and 19 percent in the 'normal' GSP tariff). In all these cases, particularly high proportions of the overall tariff quotas were allocated to Benelux and Britain on cocoa butter[18], and to Britain alone on instant coffee and pineapple chunks.[19] Once again, the three new members were entitled to adjust their duty rates upwards by only 20 percent on canned pineapples – which meant, for example, that Malaysian canned pineapple imported within the quota to Britain would pay only 2.4 percent in 1974.

In special trade agreements signed with India and Bangladesh, it was agreed that EEC duties on jute and coir manufactures would be cut by up to half by 1975, as long as exports from the two countries remained within specified limits. But Britain was authorised, transitionally, to continue extending the duty-free access previously available under Commonwealth preferential terms: a provision which, at least for 1974, gave the two countries one of the main trading rights for which they had been pressing during and after the negotiations for EEC enlargement.

Similarly, substantial extra tariff quotas were allocated to Britain on plywood and related products, to cater for duty-free imports from Malaysia and Singapore; and to Denmark for imports of various classes of textiles,[20] because 'the Kingdom of Denmark has for a number of years been importing relatively large quantities (of these products) and has therefore ceased to produce the articles in question'.[21]

This last provision is perhaps the most important of any of the 'special' or transitional arrangements, since it is the only case where special measures were taken to allow for trade resulting from a member state's successful industrial adjustment to continue, rather than to permit traditional trade flows to continue, as in the Malaysian plywood case.

More changes in the scheme are proposed for 1975.[22] These have three aims. First, to improve the terms for processed agricultural goods, by widening the preferential margin to 50% of mfn duties, abolishing all duties of 5% and under, and adding some new products particularly of interest to Asian countries. Second, to make access for manufactures generally easier by cutting back to a minimum the number of 'sensitive' products and transferring most of them to the less rigid surveillance of the 'semi-sensitive' category. Treatment of textiles and footwear, however, remains the same. Third, to limit access for the 'highly competitive' manufactures of Hong Kong, South Korea and Yugoslavia, in order to give other developing countries a better chance.

These provisions are discussed in Chapters 8 and 9. They do, on balance, appear to represent an improvement in the scheme. But the provisions for manufactures, at least, are approached with the extreme caution which has marked the Community's GSP policy throughout.

NOTES

1. Brussels Tariff Nomenclature. Broadly, chapters 1-24 of the BTN cover food and agricultural products: 25-99 cover mineral and manufactured products.
2. However, *most* primary products in these groups are duty-free in the Common External Tariff in any case.
3. Originally the countries covered by this proviso were Colombia, India, Jamaica, South Korea, Mexico, Pakistan and the United Arab Republic.
4. Volume in the case of textiles. (cif = cost, insurance and freight).
5. For some 'extra-sensitive' textiles the tariff quota was fixed at the volume of imports in 1968. This highly restrictive formula both prevented any growth in duty free imports and prevented advantages being gained by cheaper suppliers.
6. In the proportions Germany 37.5 percent, France 27.1 percent, Italy 20.3 percent, Benelux 15.1 percent; determined in relation to GNP, imports and population.
7. TD/B/C.5/3, p. 30, Table 1.
8. Official Journal No. L 289, Lists A to C. E.g. a minimum 60 percent of the cost of radios manufactured in ldcs must be local value added: at least half of the parts used must be of local origin: and all transistors used in manufacture must be locally produced.
9. See Chapter 8.
10. Set out in Official Journal Vol. 16, No. L 358 of 28 December 1973.
11. Replaced in December 1973 by the GATT Multifibre Textile Arrangement.
12. See Commission document COM (73) 1800 final, 24 October 1973, p.4.
13. White spirit, paraffin, fuel and lubricating oils, goatskins, plaiting materials, optical glass, locks and keys, small electric motors, bicycles, cycle parts, watch cases and record matrices.
14. Calcium carbides, regenerated cellulose, rectangles of unworked glass.
15. The division for most products on the general list, and for footwear, was W. Germany 27.5 percent, Benelux 10.5 percent, France 19 percent, Italy 15 percent, Denmark 5 percent, Ireland 1 percent, U.K. 22 percent.
16. Within a tariff quota of 21,600 tonnes.
17. Within tariff quotas.
18. 12,150 and 8,400 tonnes respectively out of a total of 21,600 for the Nine.
19. 15,900 tonnes out of 18,750 for instant coffee; 13,840 tonnes out of 20,000 for pineapple chunks.
20. Cotton yarn, graded from 14,000 to 40,000 to 50,000 metres per kg; raw cotton fabrics between 115 and 165 cm. wide and 'not specified'; yarn of continuous man-made fibres and of discontinuous synthetic fibres; sisal rope and twine.
21. Regulation 3502/73, OJ Vol.16 No. L 358, 28 December 1973.
22. See OJ Vol. 17 No. C110 of 21 September 1974

3. THE ECONOMICS OF GENERALISED PREFERENCES

Introduction

The case for the introduction of GSP tariff-cutting schemes was most authoritatively expounded by Raúl Prebisch, first Secretary-General of UNCTAD, in his preliminary report for the first UNCTAD Conference in 1964.[1] Prebisch argued that the promotion of exports of processed and manufactured goods was a potentially valuable – almost a necessary – element in ldcs' development strategies. The aim was to diversify the structure of ldc economies away from an over-concentration on exports of primary products – in general, much less dynamic than those of processed or manufactured goods – in order to enable developing countries to improve their own terms of trade, and close their imbalance in trade, *vis-à-vis* the West.

The belief that primary products in general were likely to face declining export prices, and hence that ldcs' export revenue was likely either to fall or to grow very slowly, was fundamental to the case. The demand for primary products in general was seen to be less income-elastic, and less price-elastic, than that for manufactures. Low income elasticity meant that over time demand grew only slowly in relation to income levels in the principal markets (Western countries). Low price elasticity, while implying that price cutting would not repay ldcs as a group by a compensating increase in sales volume (although one country might gain a temporary advantage by unilateral price cutting) should also have meant that a general rise in price would not cause a corresponding fall in demand. For some commodities this may be true: but for a considerable number (e.g. cotton, rubber, jute, sisal) high prices were likely to encourage substitution of synthetic for natural products, a trend which was in any case apparent during the 1960s as petrochemicals and plastics industries developed.

Although the theory of a long-term secular decline in primary prices has often been contested, it certainly appears to have been the case throughout the 1960s that their prices deteriorated relative to those of manufactures; and evidence suggests that those developing countries which did succeed in breaking away as exporters of manufactures improved their own terms of trade relative to those which did not.[2]

An equally important reason for moving into exports of processed and manufactured goods was the extra value added which an ldc would gain, together with any extra employment which new industries might provide. To the extent that industrialisation was important for development (in providing additional production and employment) export-biased industrialisation – with the incentive of international competition to encourage competitiveness – was a means of providing both national product and foreign exchange.

Access to Western markets was obviously likely to be important to developing countries hoping to promote exports of manufactures and processed goods. Reductions in tariff barriers – although not by any means a full solution to problems of access – would be an essential part. But Prebisch went further than arguing for free access to developed countries markets, in suggesting that preferential terms would be necessary if the required break-through were to be made. This proposition, while perhaps true in some cases, is debatable in others; and discriminatory preferential access terms may not even have much meaning for some products and some import markets. This chapter attempts to distinguish the case for *free* access to Western markets from that for *preferential* terms for ldcs at large.

Historical perspective

The word 'preference' conveys the idea of discriminating in favour of one party at the expense of another.

Historically, trading preferences were typically extended by metropolitan countries to their colonies (e.g. Britain's Imperial and later Commonwealth preferences, or French preferences for goods from Francophone Africa) as a means of developing trade between the colony and the metropole, of encouraging metropolitan investors to develop and exploit colonial resources, and of ensuring that colonial exports would be directed to the metropole and not elsewhere. The preferential networks created by European colonialism strengthened direct, parallel ties between colonial and metropolitan countries and discouraged cross-frontier trade between colonies of different metropolitan powers or trade between colonies and other metropolitan (or non-colonising) Western countries.

Although such preferences were as much a reflection of political connections as of economic conditions, they were of considerable value to those developing countries which benefited from them. These countries were (and are) reluctant to see them abolished. The question of how to treat products and countries situated inside the various ex-colonial preferential networks has been a live issue in many debates on changes in developed countries' trade policy – particularly, on the one hand, in the discussion of the effects of British entry to the EEC, and on the other, in the introduction of

GSP schemes.

Infant Industries

The encouragement of new, infant industries has been a mainstay of the case for preferences.

> 'The case for preferential treatment for exports of developing countries is that it would help the industries of developing countries to overcome the difficulties that they encounter in export markets because of their high initial costs. It is a temporary measure which, by opening up larger markets to the industries of developing countries, would enable them to lower their costs and thus compete on world markets without the need for continuing preference'.[3]

The infant industry case is based on three arguments: first, of increasing returns to scale (as output grows, unit costs diminish up to the point at which the industry is competitive); second, of 'externalities' (the growth in an economy of secondary industries, services and infrastructure investment around a newly established development): third, of its learning effect in the development of technical, organisational and managerial skills. In the development of home-based industries, the infant industry argument is generally used to justify tariffs on imports or subsidies on domestic output, aimed at altering the balance between the price of home and foreign goods in favour of domestic production in order that producers can operate profitably until the point at which average unit costs of production are low enough to compete on the domestic market without a tariff. As long as the particular industry involved does actually become efficient enough to allow the abolition of the import duty, an infant industry tariff is equivalent to a temporary subsidy paid by consumers to producers. Professor Harry Johnson has described the process as a 'social investment' in return for which a country 'acquired an industry able to compete at world market prices while the producers earn higher incomes than they would have earned without the social investment.'[4]

A tariff preference in an import market can also be seen as a subsidy – in this case, of producers in the exporting country. If, after a preferential tariff cut is made, the market price of the good remains the same and extra profits are passed back to the exporter, the importing country as a whole is subsidising the foreign producer through lost tariff revenue which would otherwise have been charged. If the market price does fall, either immediately or over time, consumers in the importing country gain, but previously protected domestic producers lose to the extent that imports replace domestic production or supply any new demand created. Fear that this may happen is what creates such strong (and often successful) pressure against preferences by 'sensitive' industries in developed countries.

The infant industry case also implies that preferences should be phased out as industries become competitive on world markets. Prebisch suggested that preferences should be introduced, in respect of any one industry in any one developing country, for 'a period of no less than ten years'[5] after which preferential treatment would be withdrawn unless it could be shown acceptably that special circumstances justified its continuation. This would encourage entrepreneurs to make sure that the industries set up were fully competitive by the time the shelter of preferences was withdrawn; and, if the ten-year period for each industry were counted from the time at which it was established, those which were established later 'would enjoy preferential treatment not merely in relation to the industries of developed countries but also in relation to those of the more advanced developing countries, once the respective industries of the latter countries were no longer entitled to preferences'.[6] Conceived in this way, the ten-year term could be used as a partial solution to one of the main problems raised by ldcs in considering the design of the GSP – that of giving especially favourable treatment to the least developed countries. But such a system would also have made the administration of the GSP even more complex.

Temporary preferences can be seen in two ways. First they may imply an acceptance that some measure of protection against outside suppliers is the norm in any developed economy and that the measure of international competitiveness is whether an exporting industry can compete effectively with protected home producers. Johnson has again put the point neatly: 'Preferences are therefore justifiable, in general terms, if there is some reason for regarding the countries suggested for preference as more like residents than other foreigners . . . or for regarding them as more worthy than other foreigners . . . In short, a protectionist regards preferences as a legitimate gesture of friendship'.[7]

Preferences in their protectionist framework thus entail the re-imposition of tariffs on industries which become competitive or, more broadly, on developing countries which reach a certain stage of industrialisation or competitiveness. The Brasseur plan[8] would, if introduced, have been just such a scheme. But this approach is also evident in the various GSP schemes actually introduced – in the selective exclusion of sensitive products or of a few particularly competitive countries (e.g. Hong Kong) or in conditions placed on the extension of preferences on particular items (e.g. the connection of EEC tariff preferences for jute manufactures from India and Bangladesh with 'voluntary export limitation' undertakings by the two countries).

Secondly, preferences may also be temporary where trade barriers are being generally reduced or abolished. Their elimination would come about through all exports being put on the same free trade, rather than protectionist, footing. They would be given in advance of general trade liberalisation.

This view was put forward particularly by British and German delegates to UNCTAD I, in arguing that tariff preferences for developing countries should be treated as an advance stage in the general reduction of tariffs which was expected to result from the Kennedy Round of negotiations in GATT. The original aim of these negotiations had been to cut tariffs across the board by 50 percent from the level prevailing in 1963, as well as to reduce the number and incidence of non-tariff barriers to trade. An immediate cut in tariffs of 50 percent for developing countries' exports would probably have given a significant short-term cost advantage; duty-free terms of access would have given a preferential advantage which would remain even if the Kennedy Round had achieved its stated ends in full.

In the event, as is well known, it did not fulfil its expectations. The average reduction in rates of tariff was some 30 percent; non-tariff barriers, including 'voluntary' export limitation agreements, were not dealt with; and, as Balassa has shown,[9] the tariffs imposed by most Western countries on the imports from ldcs, considered in terms of either nominal or effective protection rates, remained generally higher than those on goods mainly traded among developed countries. Developing countries therefore still had, even after the Kennedy Round, an interest in the preferential reduction of trade barriers.

Do Preferences Mean Anything In the EEC Context?

Preferential access is, of course, not the main issue where the problem is that of competition between imports and similar goods produced in the importing country. Insofar as tariffs and other trade barriers imposed by any one country or trade group are intended to protect domestic production from *any* outside competition, the problem for trading partners, including ldcs, is rather to gain reasonable terms under which their goods can enter the domestic market. Reductions in trade barriers are important to create trade: preferential terms for a particular group of traders (e.g. those in ldcs) benefit that group by diverting trade from others.

The EEC presents a particularly pointed example of the 'access versus preferences' question. The reduction of barriers to trade within the Community has led intra-Community trade to grow much more rapidly than trade with countries outside the area.

TABLE 3.1

EEC EXTRA- AND INTRA-TRADE 1960, 1970, 1972
(U.S. $m fob)

	1960	1970	1972
Intra-Community trade	10,250	43,300	61,550
Exports to all other countries	19,480	45,210	62,030
Imports from all other countries	18,030	41,960	52,730
Exports to ldcs	6,645	11,410	15,000
Imports from ldcs	6,225	13,810	18,240
Total exports } including intra-Community	29,730	88,510	123,580
Total imports } including intra-Community	28,280	85,260	114,280
Balance with all other countries	+ 1,450	+ 3,250	+ 9,300
Balance with ldcs	+ 420	- 2,400	- 3,240

Source: *International Trade, 1972,* GATT, Geneva 1973

Freedom of trade within the Community means that preference for third-country supplies over goods produced in any EEC countries is impossible, and the wider the enlargement of the Community the less scope there is for preferential access.

Before EEC enlargement, GSP access to the Community of Six meant that ldc products eligible for GSP terms gained a margin of tariff preference against goods from EFTA countries, Eastern Europe (disregarding bilateral agreements) and other developed countries, including the United States, Japan, Australia and South Africa. Between 1960 and 1972, ldcs' share of total imports into the Six from non-members fell only very slightly, and in fact rose between 1970 and 1972. The introduction of the GSP may have contributed to the increase. Community enlargement and the free trade area in manufactures with the remaining EFTA countries, however, have eroded the preferential value of duty-free access under the GSP by freeing trade in GSP goods between the original Six and the three new members (in both directions) and between the Six and the remaining EFTA countries from tariff and other impediments to trade. Ldcs' exports of goods counted as non-sensitive under the GSP to the Nine and EFTA are, under these circumstances, traded under the same terms as Community and EFTA products; but exports of sensitive products, subject to ceiling limitations under the GSP, will face a degree of discrimination against them. The value of *preferential* duty-free access of ldcs then relates solely to goods in which their main competition in European markets comes from non-European developed market-economy countries or from socialist states.

In 1973, the UNCTAD secretariat, as part of its review of GSP schemes, published a study[10] in which an estimate was made of the proportion of ldc exports to the Nine which might be said, in these terms, to be able to benefit from preferential access under the GSP. Broadly, the study concluded that some 76 percent by value of the imports into the enlarged Community of GSP products (excluding petroleum products and leather goods for statistical reasons) would, in 1970, have entered duty-free from Western European sources, if the enlarged Community's trading arrangements had been in force at the time. The inference which must be drawn from this is that, for GSP products, the ldcs' main competition in Community markets comes from preferred Western European sources, rather than from countries which are not treated preferentially or from other ldcs.

One may conclude from this that the maintenance of preferential terms over other developed countries (particularly Japan) is likely to be of secondary (though significant) importance compared with the ability to compete effectively with European manufactures. Access, therefore, is more important for the majority of GSP products than preferential margins; and the limitation of GSP access by tariff quotas is likely to be, in this context, a serious handicap to the development of ldcs' trade in any product which may be regarded as 'sensitive'.

NOTES

1. *Towards a New Trade Policy for Development,* UN, 1964.
2. See GATT, *International Trade* (1970) pp. 11-14.
3. *Towards a New Trade Policy, op. cit.* p.65
4. H. G. Johnson, *Economic Policies towards Less Developed Countries,* George Allen and Unwin, 1964, p. 181.
5. *Towards a New Trade Policy, op. cit.* p.69
6. *Ibid.*, p. 70.
7. H. G. Johnson, *op. cit.* p. 200
8. See pp. 39-43
9. UNCTAD Paper TD/6/Rev.1 *The Kennedy Round: Estimated Effects on Trade Barriers,* Geneva, 1968.
10. TD/B/C.5/8 *Effects of enlargement of the European Community on the Generalised System of Preferences.* Geneva, March 1973

4. THE COMMUNITY AT WORK

The Institutional Structure

The institutions of the European Community and their main functions are set out in Figure 4.1. This study, however, is less concerned with the details of how the institutions operate than with the role which each plays in foreign affairs affecting the Community and its member states, and the channels of influence which exist for sectoral, national and external points of view to make themselves felt. It is particularly relevant here to look at the ways in which developing countries can make their ideas and their demands known in Community circles.

The Council and the Commission:

The Council of Ministers

At the heart of the Community as a political entity are the Council of Ministers and the Commission. The Council is the final decision-making and legislative body of the Community; nothing can become Community law unless it has been approved by the Council. Formally, it consists of one Minister from each member state; the EEC Commission is represented at meetings, but Commissioners are not members of the Council. In practice, there are several 'Councils', depending on the subject-matter, Foreign Ministers of the member states generally 'leading' in General Councils and others operating in Council meetings which affect their departmental responsibilities.[1] The chair is taken by each member state in 'absolute' alphabetical order[2] for six months at a time. During any Minister's presidency, a separate Minister or senior official must represent the national point of view as spokesman; the President of the Council is intended to be a 'Community man' rather than represent a national view, although, inevitably, conduct of Council business can be tempered by the attitudes and views of the current President.

Council decisions on any matters which affect significant national interests must be unanimous. Other issues may be decided by simple or qualified majorities. The range of decisions on which unanimity is necessary has grown markedly. Now, any questions which would lead to a change in a principle of policy, and some matters of detailed, though important, policy administration (notably price regulations under the Common Agricultural Policy) have to be decided unanimously.

Figure 4.1 **Working Structure of the European Community**

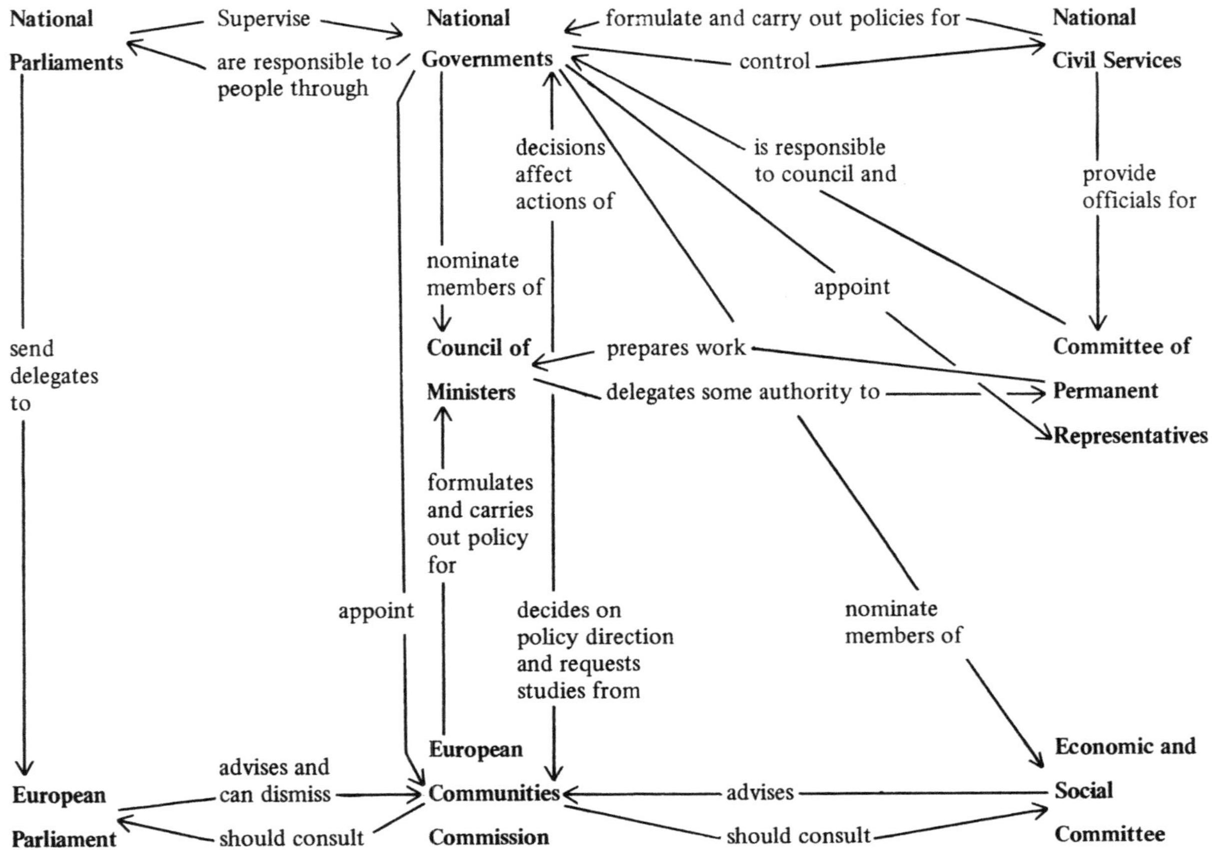

The unanimity rule puts a premium on compromise among Community members and reinforces the importance of the member states against the Commission. This was borne out both by France's dominance in Community affairs up to 1973 and by the more recent renegotiation period in which the British Labour government has sought to change, or at least redefine, many Community policies and attitudes. Support from other member states is essential.

The work of the Council is supported by a strong hierarchy of committees and working groups, headed by the Committee of Permanent Representatives (COREPER) which brings together the chief representatives of the member states in a Community setting. Noel[3] notes that the Committee, like the Council, has a dual responsibility; to be 'representatives of the Member States' and to be 'members of the Council' i.e. of a Community institution with wider aims, at least in theory, than the pursuit of national goals. Although powers of decision are not formally delegated from the Council to the Committee, whose powers are in principle limited to 'prepare the work of the Council and carry out the latter's mandates',[4] in practice the Committee and its sub-groups settle a large majority of the more routine, or less politically sensitive, decisions to be made by the Council, which are then normally rubberstamped by the Council itself. But the Council retains the right to discuss any question 'prepared' by the Committee.

Beneath COREPER, more than 130 subcommittees and working parties work 'in the framework of' the Council. These may be composed of officials from the Permanent Representatives' offices, or of home civil servants seconded as experts on particular topics, or of a mixture of the two. These committees undertake the day-by-day work of the Council. 'As a general rule any new question referred to the Council is automatically sent to the competent working party by the Chairman of the Committee of Permanent Representatives. The Committee only handles it on a report from the working party, and it reaches the Council's agenda only when the preparatory work in the Committee has been concluded'.[5]

The work of the Council and its committees is limited in two main ways. First, all its actions must be within the areas defined by the Treaties of Paris and Rome which set up the European Coal and Steel Community, Euratom and the Economic Community. Second, all its decisions, except in a few very narrowly defined areas (such as the terms of reference which will be given to the Commission for negotiations) are taken on the basis of Commission proposals. The function of the Committees and working groups have been described (in another context) as to 'haggle over it (a Commission proposal) and amend it as necessary in order to obtain a text which is acceptable to all the Governments concerned. This is a process which has in the past taken anything between six months and several years, and by the end of it the draft may well have been changed out of all recognition'.[6]

Formally, the former restriction on Council activity may be set aside if the Council decides unanimously, on a proposal from the Commission, to take action of a type not specifically provided for, in the treaties, in order to attain a 'Community' objective. In principle this provision opens the door to a wide interpretation of the Community's joint activities. In practice, however, the scope of the Community's political operations has been closely circumscribed by the interpretation set on the Treaties by the member states; in particular, before Community enlargement, by that of France which, according to one commentator, had taken the view that in signing the Treaty of Rome it accepted a number of limited commitments about the way in which certain named aspects of economic policy were to be run.

So far, the member states have held firmly to the right to take the main political decisions on the directions in which Community policy ought to move, setting on the shoulders of the Commission the responsibility for ensuring that political directions are translated into action. At the highest level this type of progress has been made through a series of 'Summit' meetings of heads of government of the member states: in the Hague in 1969, to discuss *inter alia* the question of British entry and, in outline, the concept of European economic and monetary union; in Paris in 1972; and in Copenhagen in December 1973. These meetings have taken place unfettered by constraints placed on meetings of the Council of Ministers by a restrictive interpretation of the Treaty of Rome; although even here a clear distinction tends to have been drawn on what are or are not Community responsibilities in the formal sense. Thus the communiqué of the Summit conference of the Nine held in October 1972, in discussing the development of 'an overall policy of development cooperation on a world-wide scale'[7] resorted to inviting 'the Institutions of the Community and Member States',[8] to study questions of trade relations with developing countries (a Community responsibility) and of volume and conditions of official aid (a national responsibility, except for the European Development Fund.

The practical result of this was, over time, to create a general discussion of development policy through a series of intergovernmental working parties, which resulted in the acceptance, in principle, that Community aid might be extended to non-associates.[9]

The second limitation ensures the permanence of the 'dialogue' which exists between the Council and its subsidiary organs and the

EEC Commission.

The Communities' Commission

The formal structure of the Commission has frequently been described and analysed.[10] Briefly, it consists (since EEC enlargement) of thirteen Commissioners,[11] two each from France, West Germany, Italy and the UK and one each from Belgium, Denmark, Eire, Luxembourg and the Netherlands, nominated by their national governments for four-year terms of office. Although nationally appointed, the Commissioners are required to act completely independently of national considerations and in the wider 'Community' interest. Each one has the right to appoint his own personal *cabinet* of advisers and co-negotiators, who are usually (but not always) people of the Commissioner's own nationality and who act both as a political intelligence service for the Commissioners and as negotiators, where necessary, on the Commissioners' behalf and with their full authority. The Commission itself has a working staff of about 5,000, mostly appointed within a national quota system. It has twenty departments (Directorates-General), the staff of each of which is headed by a Director-General who will, usually, be of different nationality from the relevant Commissioner, the aim being to ensure that no particular national interest comes to dominate any field of policy within the Commission.[12]

Relations with developing countries are covered by two separate departments: Directorate General I (External Relations) and DG VIII (Development and Cooperation). Within DG I, one directorate covers relations with developing countries in Latin America and Asia (except the Middle and Far East) the UN economic agencies other than UNCTAD, and the GSP. The same directorate is charged with coordinating policies with DG VIII. A separate directorate covers, *inter alia,* relations with Middle Eastern and Far Eastern countries. DG VIII, in turn, is required to deal with all general questions of development policy, relations with Africa and with the Southern and Eastern Mediterranean, trade promotion, food aid, commodity agreements and general questions concerning UNCTAD, other than the GSP. This awkward-looking division of responsibilities, which appears to work fairly well in practice, has evolved from a fairly strict division, before Community enlargement, between relations with Associates (DG VIII) and those with other developing countries (DG 1 and the former DG XI, External Trade). But the prime responsibility for the GSP rests with DG.1

The most important functions of the Commission, as far as this study is concerned, are initiating or proposing new policies for the

Community which are consistent with the Treaty of Rome and steering these proposals through the Council bodies, to develop 'European' or 'communautaire' policies on which member states can agree. The ability to initiate measures which may eventually become Community legislation has probably, so far, been the most important of the Commission's formal powers. Without Commission proposal as a formal starting point the Council of Ministers may be unable to decide, as David Coombes has argued, on 'provisions which are at all general in scope or of major importance.[13]

But although a Commission proposal formally begins the process of policy determination, the political starting point may lie with either the Commission or – frequently – the member states. A Commission 'initiative' in any area may in fact be a reaction to, or a development of, national policies; moreover, these need not necessarily be first expounded through the Community medium of the Council of Ministers. Each of the Nine has its own foreign policy objectives. Each of them is a member of international organisations – e.g. OECD, GATT, NATO, the United Nations – through which these aims are pursued. It has been fairly rare in the past for the member states to follow an agreed Community line in the day-to-day work of these organisations, although consultation and coordination are gradually increasing[14] and the Commission will usually attempt to work out a common attitude; rather, as will be seen in the case of the generalised preference scheme, even where an issue crosses the frontier between strictly 'national' and strictly 'Community' responsibilities, the wider fora of OECD and the United Nations may serve to reveal the differences of view among the members, and act as places where intra-Community bargains are worked out.

The basic question of whether or not generalised preferences should be extended was largely settled in discussions in and around the OECD and UNCTAD. The Community institutions appear to have taken a back seat until the basic issue was fairly well along the road to settlement. Once the political issue of principle had been cleared up, however, the internal process of 'dialogue' between Commission and Council on the more technical issue of *how* a preference scheme should be designed got under way.

But what are the aims of the Community institutions – in particular the Commission – in this 'dialogue'? The first point to remember is that the Commission itself is not a monolith; like any other civil service, it is a collection of departments and sections whose interests often conflict. Although policy proposals are presented to the Council of Ministers in the name of the whole Commission, the Commissioner in whose department they have been prepared takes responsibility for steering them through Council debates; and although proposals are debated by the whole Commission, they need not be unanimously approved. Compromise, therefore, plays a less important part in Commission than in Council proceedings.

The main aims which the Commission must always bear in mind are the creation of joint policies and the promotion of a common political entity. It attempts to mediate in Council debates with the aim of 'upgrading the common interest'[15] among the differing national policies of the Nine. Its ability to do so, however, depends on the extent to which the member governments are willing to go along with new Commission proposals; and, in the period preceding enlargement, the strong hold of the Council – and, at the political level, the member states' governments acting outside the Council structure – on the reins of the Community, meant that the Commission's scope for pursuing its idea of the common interest was very much restricted. One field in which the Commission had a definite role, however, was in the creation of a single Community market through the removal of domestic barriers to internal trade, and this explains, to a large extent, why the Commission has sometimes appeared – particularly immediately before EEC enlargement – to have been obsessed with the need for 'harmonisation' of relative *minutiae* such as the definitions of bread and beer.

Without the active support of the member states for the extension of Community jurisdiction over national bailiwicks, the Commission's mediative role – of bringing together diverse national views – gains more importance than its ability to 'upgrade' the common interest. If it can create new 'European' policies at all, it may do so only by gradually eroding the areas where national governments assert their independence, and thus enlarging the number of issues which member states are prepared to allow as 'Community' matters. At worst, the Commission's role may be reduced to merely seeking *any* compromise which can be found of members' demands and desires.

The Commission took an active part in pursuing and promoting policy initiatives until the internal crisis of 1965. Indeed, the activity of the Commission as a political force was one of the main immediate causes of that crisis. From then until the enlargement of the Community, the Commission adopted a much more defensive attitude to bargaining and compromise, to square with the greater emphasis placed on unanimity among Council members where important national issues were at stake. Since enlargement, with a number of new Commissioners of considerable political weight and new policy initiatives, broadly determined in Summit meetings, to be taken in the agricultural, trade and regional fields, the Commission has again become more activist.

The European Parliament and the Economic and Social Committee.

The European Parliament is the nearest approach to popular representation at Community level. However, its 198 members are not directly elected[16] but appointed from among the members of the Parliaments of the EEC member states; it has, as yet, few powers to decide any issue of policy, and cannot over-rule Council decisions.

The Parliament can dismiss the EEC Commission *en bloc* on a two-thirds majority of votes cast and a simple majority of the entire membership,[17] but cannot participate in the appointment of a new Commission, which is the responsibility of the national governments.[18] So far, however, this power has never been used.

In the legislative field, the Parliament is generally (but not necessarily) consulted by the Council on Commission proposals; and as long as the Council has not made a final decision, the Commission may (and often does) change its ideas to follow Parliament's advice. The detailed examination of Commission proposals is done in Parliamentary committees, of which there are currently twelve. 'The usual procedure is for the Committee concerned, if necessary after consultation with other interested Committees, to produce a report incorporating a draft resolution. This is then considered in a plenary session . . . before the opinion of the Parliament is formally transmitted to the Council'.[19] Early consultation by the Commission with Parliamentary committees can give the Parliament a responsible role in the decision-making process; but one of the Parliament's main problems is that it is often not consulted early enough to make any great difference. The Védel report noted that even the consultative function of the Parliament was weakened 'by the fact that, although the Commission seeks the support of the Parliament, it enters into negotiations with the Council, even before submitting its formal proposals to the latter. It is always difficult for a parliamentary body to be associated with negotiations, even in a consultative capacity. Sometimes, when faced with an implicit prior agreement between the Commission and the Council, the Parliament feels that its opinion can be of no substantial significance'.[20] Parliamentary scrutiny of Commission proposals also operates through oral and written questions to the Commission, including a regular question-time (instituted in 1973) which Commissioners, who are formally responsible to the Parliament, are obliged to attend.

The Parliament's main weakness, however, is its lack of any control over the Council of Ministers. 'Although the members of the Council represent democratically elected governments, the Council itself has no parliamentary mandate, nor are its decisions subject to parliamentary ratification, either at the national or the Community level'.[21] Once a decision is made by the Council, the Parliament is powerless to change it except through encouraging the Commission to put up new proposals.

The main field in which Parliamentary powers are initially likely to be strengthened is its control over the EEC budget, which is due to be financed directly from import duties and levies and from VAT receipts by 1975. Parliament, Commission and Council have been engaged in a long and often acrimonious debate over budgetary scrutiny and approval by Parliament since 1970, when the new budgetary financing method was first agreed by the Six. Broadly, it was proposed that new expenditure in the Community budget should be subject to Parliamentary acceptance and that any disagreements between the Council and the Parliament should be ironed out in a joint committee in which the two bodies would be equally represented and in which the Commission would participate. Although this would not give the Parliament final control over 'expenditure arising automatically from treaty or other agreements already in effect' (most notably agricultural payments) it would provide an important first step in Parliamentary control of Community spending.

The catch, of course, is that even these proposals must be approved by the Council of Ministers, which could block any progress in this direction. The only sanction which the Parliament would then have would be to dismiss the Commission – a step which would not be easily taken.

The Economic and Social Committee's role is solely to give expert advice to the Council on Commission proposals. It is intended to show 'public opinion' in the Community decision-making process – at least as exemplified by an amalgam of social and economic interest groups – and to draw together sources of expert advice in different fields. The Committee has now 144 members, appointed as representatives of the various categories of economic and social life, in particular, 'representatives of producers, agriculturalists, transport operators, workers, merchants, artisans, the liberal professions and the general interest'.[22] In practice the ESC has divided up into groups representing employers, workers and 'other interests': and these groups have become built into the operation of the ESC to the extent that national appointments try to balance the three groups equally. (Whether this actually represents a reasonable balance of opinion and interest is open to question.) The Committee also divides up into specialised sections and study groups covering particular topics: at present there are nine sections.[23] Members of the ESC can choose, largely according to their own interests, in which sections they will take part. The Committee may, but need not in most cases, be consulted by the Council or the

Commission: it can take the initiative in raising matters on which it has not been consulted.

Both the Parliament and the Committee can affect Community decisions materially if they make their opinions felt early enough in the process of policy making, (although the Council and the Commission can accept or reject their ideas largely as they wish). The time factor can be very important: it is of little use to seek Parliamentary and ESC opinions when policy on a particular issue is all but finally settled. On the GSP, the ESC was apparently not consulted at all; the Parliament, not until 1971, when the form and content of the Community's preference scheme were almost entirely fixed both internally and internationally.

Pressures and Influences on Community Authorities

Community policy is not made in a vacuum. It has to be worked out in the face of many national, sectoral and international pressures and constraints. This section aims to outline briefly what these are likely to be and how they are expressed; Chapter 7 will look at the pressures which actually influenced the Commission and Council in setting up the GSP, and the directions in which the Community organs were moved by their influence.

Pre-existing Community policy

Apart from major new departures, such as the decision to form an economic and monetary union taken at a Summit meeting of the original Six in 1969 – and even this was foreseen in the Treaty of Rome – Community policy has developed very largely stage-by-stage according to precedent. Generally speaking, it would be inconsistent for the Commission not to defend policies which it had steered through the Council of Ministers; to a lesser extent, the member states are likely to feel committed to agreed policies (at least during the period of any one government) and to defend the existing state of affairs in the Community against attacks from outside. The existence of 'European' policies in particular areas is likely to temper any new proposals which may affect these policies and the Commission will have to take into account the constraints of existing policies in drawing up its own memoranda. But circumstances and political attitudes change with time; and as an area of EEC policy develops disagreement may arise among the member states and within the Commission on the effects and administration of the policy (e.g. the longstanding debate about reform of the Common Agricultural Policy). However, as the CAP debate shows, it is difficult to make radical changes in an existing policy where even one country's national interests are strongly involved in supporting it (partly at least because of the unanimity rule applied by the Council). New proposals thus are constrained by existing policies; and the strength of the constraints will depend very much on how adamantly members are prepared to defend the existing set-up.

National Policies

The aims pursued by the governments of the member states are a key factor in Community decisions, because of the determining role of the Council and its unanimity rule. Similarly, the Community's existing policies feed back into national politics:

> 'Policy-making at the national level was already a complex process, and membership of the Community has overlaid this with new constraints. The gradual expansion of Community activities has affected a range of sectors and responsibilities hitherto confined to the sphere of national governments. Each government has to work to the deadlines imposed by the Community timetable, at the same time taking account of the pressures which stem from its domestic environment.'[24]

The different governments of the member states have looked on the 'Community dimension' of their policies in different ways, reflecting their objectives in the Community, with the French attitude apparently more consistent in the past than others. But national policy is not monolithic, either. Political and departmental objectives may conflict and areas of policy which have become, wholly or partly, Community responsibilities may conflict with those held primarily in national hands; functional needs increasingly cut across national interests. 'Ministries within each government have varying attitudes on the objectives to be pursued at the Community level . . . There is therefore, not always an uncontested national interest around which positions for Community negotiations can be built.'[25] Moreover, policies change both with governments (e.g. the difference in attitude to Community policies between Tory and Labour governments in Britain) and in response to domestic and international circumstances.

The field of foreign affairs is one where Community and national responsibilities particularly overlap. This is even more the case in the area of external trade policy. Where the Community has formal responsibility for an area of policy (e.g. tariff negotiations) the Commission can, and usually does, conduct business for the Community. David Coombes's detailed case study of the role of the Commission in the Kennedy Round negotiations has illustrated, however, how far its freedom of action is limited by the Council:

'Very early on, the Commission took its stand on three basic principles . . . (which) formed part of the recommendation which the

Commission made to the Council of Ministers in December 1963 for a mandate to open the negotiations in accordance with Article 111 of the Treaty of Rome. The mandate finally adopted by the Council differed little from the Commission's draft and it has even been said that the final negotiating position of the Community in 1967 was very similar to this original mandate of 1963 . . . But up to the middle of 1966 the Commission was given very little discretion with which to negotiate. Progress was often halted while the Commission waited for necessary renewal or re-interpretation of its mandate from the Council of Ministers. In the earlier stages not all the member states were entirely willing to be represented by the Commission and some made direct approaches of their own to the other GATT partners'.[26]

Sectoral Pressures[27]

National policy making is perpetually subject to varying degrees and directions of pressure from all sectors of opinion and of the economy: from farmers, consumers, trade unions, various sectors of industry, research foundations, MPs representing constituency, regional or welfare interests, the press, and the electorate directly. Sources of pressure may become institutionalised in professional, voluntary or *ad hoc* bodies representing particular interests – e.g. in Britain the National Farmers' Union, the Consumers' Association, the TUC, the CBI, the Engineering Employers' Federation – and temporary alliances may be formed to defend, or promote, common interests.

At Community level, national pressure groups have combined in 'European' federations to maintain contact with the Commission, which does not, as a principle, keep official contact with national groups. In some fields the views of pressure groups are transmitted through official committees meeting under the auspices of the Commission. Currently, such consultative committees exist for areas covered by the Coal and Steel Community, for Euratom, and for agricultural, transport, labour, social and consumer affairs. This last was established only in September 1973, and links the Commission's Environment and Consumer Protection Service with a new federation of consumer associations. Previously the 'consumer interest' had no voice at Community level. But even without the formality of consultative committees, interest groups organised at a 'European' level may submit memoranda to and seek consultations with Commissioners and their officials; and such channels of communication are very active.

There is no *a priori* reason why the national organisations of particular interest groups should share a common interest in particular Community policies. Pressures through Brussels-based federations may be supported by national action aimed at the Council via governments;

equally, national organisations may press governments to block Commission proposals with which they disagree. Similarly, individual industries or unions (such as the textile industries or the miners' unions) may keep up their own channels of communication with the Commission independently of federations.[28]

The Economic and Social Committee is the other main direct channel through which interest groups can influence the Community authorities. The division of the ESC into 'employers', 'workers', and 'other interests' – a far more diverse group than the first two would seem to be – has been noted. But although national representation on the ESC tends to be well coordinated, and the strength of the Community farm lobby also shows itself in ESC committees and study groups, the Committee is unlikely to be a consistent channel of influence for any one interest. Its groups generally cover the range of interests represented, and the need to achieve a consensus on any given subject promotes compromise and means that no sectoral interest is likely consistently to gain the upper hand.

Communications with Developing Countries

In external affairs, the Community's susceptibility to pressures from outside sources is partly determined by its own institutional ties, but probably more, once again, by the policies and susceptibilities of the member states. It has already been noted that all the EEC members are members of the relevant international organisations. In many of these (e.g. the UN organisations, OECD) the Commission is represented separately as a member or an observer.

The Community, as an entity, has its own diplomatic existence. It maintains delegations abroad, and foreign countries maintain missions in Brussels accredited to the Community as embassies in national capitals. The number of developing countries with missions to the Community has, moreover, greatly expanded with EEC enlargement and the Community's commitments to the expansion of Association and to a wider development policy.

Associates of the Community have a particularly close institutional connection with the Brussels network though the Association Council, at Ministerial level, and the Association Committee, at official level. Formally, Associates have the right to be consulted on any proposed Community measure which affects their interests – in particular their preferential trading connections with the Community – and they make sure that their right is used. The more 'French' of the Francophone Associates have also used their influence and standing with the French government, and the importance which France has in the past attached to the maintenance of the franc zone and to French influence in Africa, as a lever to keep the Community's priority commitment to the maintenance and strengthening of Association. In the GSP debate, as will be seen, this was an important argument, particularly for restricting tariff concessions on processed agricultural goods – although it also served as a convenient peg on which to hang the interests of domestic food-processing industries in the member states. The enlargement of association, of course, greatly increases the number of countries which can make use of these special established channels of communication. But the way in which they are used is likely to change considerably – if the progress of the Association negotiations of 1974 are any guide – and, with the Giscard d'Estaing government, France also appears to be less concerned with the preservation of the Francophone connection in its old form.

Most other developing countries must rely on their normal diplomatic representation, individually or in groups,[29] to make their views known to the Community. But some have concluded bilateral agreements with the EEC which include joint standing committees on relations between them: India and Brazil are two of the most recent cases. Clearly, if the Community is prepared to be receptive to arguments advanced in these joint committees, they will provide a useful direct channel of communication. But their real value to the ldcs concerned will, partly at least, depend on the priorities which the Community itself attaches in future to different aspects of development policy – particularly to the maintenance and strengthening of Association. At present, they do not have the formal status of the Association institutions; they are, like the Association Committee, diplomatic and official, but unlike the Council of Association, not ministerial. Whether this will be a handicap remains to be seen.

'Concessions' and Burden-sharing

The discussions between the developed and developing countries in UNCTAD concerning the GSP cannot really be called true negotiations; there was no real trading of interests between 'donor' and 'recipient' countries. The ldcs – to the dismay of developed countries – pressed the view that the GSP discussions were real negotiations, in the hope that an agreement based on negotiation would be binding on donor countries; and it is possible that the ldcs saw, as a trade-off for substantial concessions in a well-designed preferential system, the removal of the pressure they exerted on the developed countries in UNCTAD. The developed countries, in turn, presented the issue simply as one of giving unilateral concessions to exporters from developing countries. In this way it could be put in terms of increasing the 'burden' of imports on their own economies.

It is evident that the balance of 'burdens' shared between the EEC and the other main 'donor' countries, in particular the USA, was watched extremely carefully. (Chapters 5 & 6 trace the progress of the negotiations around this issue.) There was, however, a counterweight to the burden-sharing issue, which affected the Community's attitude; the desire to be seen in a politically favourable light in international circles and particularly by the less-developed world. Judging by the Commission's attitudes within the Community and in the international negotiations (for want of a better word), this weighed fairly strongly in favour of the principle of GSP, at least, for the Commission; and, over time, the Commission worked consistently for the principle and for the early introduction of a scheme. And the Commission, speaking on behalf of the Community, takes not a little pride in having been the first 'donor' to introduce its GSP scheme.

NOTES

1. On this subject, see in particular Helen Wallace, *National Governments and the European Communities,* Chatham House/PEP 1973, Chapter 3.
2. i.e. in the enlarged Community Belgie/Belgique, Bundesrepublik Deutschlands, Denmark, France, Italia, Ireland, Luxembourg, Nederland, UK.
3. Emile Noel, 'The Committee of Permanent Representatives', *Journal of Common Market Studies,* V:3, March 1967.
4. Council of Ministers, Provisional Rules of Procedure, Article 16.
5. Noel, *op. cit.*
6. S. W. Fremantle, 'Removing technical barriers to trade within the Community', *European Communities Commentary No. 1,* Supplement to *Trade and Industry,* HMSO, June 1973.
7. Cmnd 5199, October 1972
8. *ibid.*
9. This was accepted by the Council in July 1974.
10. Before Community enlargement, there were nine.
11. See e.g. R. Mayne *The Institutions of the European Community* Chatham House PEP, 1968; D. Coombes, *Politics and Bureaucracy in the European Community,* Allen and Unwin/PEP, 1970; F.S. Jardine, *How the Community Works:* 'The Commission and the Council' *European Communities Commentary, op. cit.*
12. E.g. DGVIII, with a French Commissioner, has a German Director-General.
13. Coombes, *op. cit.* p.79.
14. In a crisis, however, (e.g. the oil supply crisis of winter 1973) Community co-ordination still tends to go by the board.
15. Coombes, *op. cit.* p. 251.
16. Article 138 (3) of the Treaty of Rome and has continually been a live issue.
17. Article 144 of the Treaty of Rome.

18. The Védel Committee's report (September 1972) on the future of the European Parliament recommended that the Parliament should be entitled to approve the appointment of the President of the Commission, but this recommendation has not, so far, been accepted. See *Report of the Working Party examining the problems of the enlargement of the powers of the European Parliament.* Brussels. March 1972.
19. J. F. J. Jardine, 'How the Community works: 2. The "Consultative" bodies', *European Communities Commentary, No. 2,* supplement to *Trade and Industry*, HMSO, July 1973.
20. 'The Power of the European Parliament', *European Community,* November 1973, p. 8.
21. *Report of the Working Party, op. cit.* p. 36.
22. Treaty of Rome, Article 193. (Author's underlining).
23. Agriculture; Transport and Communications; Nuclear Questions and Energy; Economic and Financial Questions; Craft and Other Industries, Trade and Services; Social Questions; External Relations; Regional Development; Protection of the Environment, Public Health and Consumption.
24. Wallace, *op. cit.* p. 17.
25. *Ibid.*
26. Coombes, *op. cit.* p. 177-8.
27. For a wide discussion of the role of pressure groups at EEC level, see D. Sidjanski, 'Pressure groups and the European Economic Community', *Government and Opposition,* Vol. 2, No. 3, 1967: J. Meynaud and D. Sidjanski, *Les groupes de pression dans la Communauté européenne,* Editions de l'Institut de Sociologie, Brussels, 1971.
28. Note that, e.g. the British National Union of Mineworkers was, until 1974 represented in Community circles, in the ECSC, despite the continuing embargo by the TUC on union participation in EEC institutions.
29. E.g. the ASEAN Brussels Committee (ABC) which promotes the mutual interests of Indonesia, Malaysia, the Philippines, Singapore and Thailand (the Association of South East Asian States)

5. HISTORY OF THE COMMUNITY GSP: SETTLING THE PRINCIPLE

Origins of the GSP: early negotiations in GATT

The principle of general preferential tariff treatment for developing countries' exports was first fully discussed internationally in GATT during 1963. In 1962 the British government (the responsible minister being Edward Heath, then President of the Board of Trade) had proposed to a Commonwealth Conference the extension of Commonwealth preferential treatment by Britain to exports from all developing countries; on condition, naturally, that other developed countries gave preferential treatment to developing countries' exports (including those of the Commonwealth).

Britain's interest in such a proposal at the time was fairly clear. As a major trading country Britain was actively concerned in the negotiations and discussions in GATT leading up to the start of the Kennedy Round of multilateral trade negotiations; and in 1962 the British government was in the middle of its first unsuccessful attempt to join the EEC. Commonwealth developing countries were still important. Many Commonwealth preferences were contractual obligations; most of the African Commonwealth countries were either just entering independence or leading up to it; and the British market was responsible for taking 22 per cent of the exports of Commonwealth developing countries. Thus, the British government felt a much greater sense of direct responsibility for Commonwealth affairs than any present-day administration would be likely to claim. From the British angle, then, the proposal had two main virtues. First, it would help to compensate Commonwealth developing countries for any losses of competitive ability they might suffer as a result of British membership of the EEC and global tariff reductions in the Kennedy Round: and secondly, it would give non-Commonwealth developing countries an 'advance' on multilateral tariff cuts, at relatively little cost to Britain in terms of revenue, while leaving the main field clear for negotiations among the major trading powers.

At the GATT ministerial meeting in May 1963, two separate proposals for special tariff treatment for developing countries were debated. The first, made as part of a Programme of Action submitted to the meeting after studies in Committee III of the GATT on obstacles to exports from developing countries, was to reduce most-favoured nation (mfn) tariffs by 50 per cent in three years for a list of semi-manufactures and manufactures of importance in the export trade of developing countries. This would have been an advance on, and might have extended, any tariff reductions in the Kennedy Round, in a non-preferential manner consistent with the GATT rules at the time; but it would have applied equally to developing and developed countries and would not, therefore, have given exporters in ldcs any discriminatory advantages.

It is clear from the Conclusions and Resolutions of the GATT ministerial meeting that no developed countries were prepared to accept this proposal outright. The majority hedged; they were prepared to 'work towards a substantial reduction of tariffs on these products' but 'action concerning the reduction of tariffs on primary products, semi-finished goods and manufactures from developing countries would come within the scope of the GATT trade negotiations' [i.e. the Kennedy Round] and, without excluding the possibility of action in advance of these negotiations (they) proposed to ensure that these products would be taken up as far as possible in their offers presented in the negotiations'.[1]

As an alternative to this, the EEC and their Associates proposed that 'special selective measures specially concerned with a view to the needs of developing countries' should be studied by a special working group. More specifically, it was at this meeting that the Belgian proposals were first put up, for selective preferences, negotiated case-by-case between developed and developing countries. These became known as the Brasseur Plan after Mr Brasseur, the Belgian Foreign Minister, who formally presented them to the GATT ministers.

The outcome of the GATT ministerial meeting, then, was only moderately satisfactory for the developing countries. No agreement could be reached on any special measures to be taken in the Kennedy Round which might benefit ldcs; and the whole question of preferences was referred back to a GATT working group. One important principle, however, was conceded: that of non-reciprocity in trade negotiations between developed and developing countries. This was set out in Paragraph 8 of the agreed conclusions of the meeting:

'In the course of the trade negotiations, no effort will be neglected to reduce obstacles to exports from less developed countries, but developed countries could not expect to benefit from reciprocity on the part of the less-developed countries.'

The question of preferences was considered by a Working Party consisting of twenty-nine members, under the chairmanship of Ambassador Miyazaki of Japan. It is interesting to note that in this group the EEC was formally represented as a Community, rather than the six governments separately; although at this stage the Community had not made up its mind corporately about the GSP idea, and there were in fact quite large differences between the member governments on the principles and the practice of preferences. Nevertheless, speaking on behalf of the member governments of the Community, the EEC representative, Mr Jean Rey, welcomed in principle 'the idea of tariff preferences to be granted on certain products with a view to stimulating industrialisation in the less-developed countries'.

It was in this meeting that the initial positions of the EEC (or at least Belgium and France), the USA, and Britain, were defined. The meeting had before it for discussion the Brasseur plan, which was presented on behalf of the EEC member governments. The United States' view was that less-developed countries could benefit from the 50 per cent across-the-board reduction in tariffs expected from the Kennedy Round, without being required to offer full reciprocity. Preferences were opposed on three grounds: that commitments to new tariff preferences to ldcs might lead partipants in the Kennedy Round negotiation to reduce the scope of their general concessions; that any new preference system would perpetuate, complicate and extend on an unequal basis existing arrangements between developed and developing countries, so that the expected benefits, if any, would go to only some ldcs; and that, in the view of the US government, ldc trade would benefit more, in the short and the long term, from non-discriminatory reduction of tariffs and elimination of non-tariff barriers, than from any programme involving the extension of new tariff preferences. The British view was that preferences should be treated, rather simply, as advance reductions in mfn rates of duty. Preferences should not either result in increases in mfn rates or hold up progress in their reduction on a non-discriminatory basis.

At this early stage, then, there were deep differences between the points of view of the main western trading nations on *whether* preferential access ought to be generally extended, and if so, *how*: with the USA strongly opposed to any departure from the mfn principle, and Britain and the EEC in support of the concept of generalised preferences but with very different ideas on how it should be put into action. Although the Brasseur plan was presented as a simple way of approaching the problem, it met with suspicion from the start, and many complicating features were brought out in discussing it.

The Brasseur Plan

The Brasseur Plan was presented first to GATT in May 1963, then to the OECD Council in its preparatory meetings for UNCTAD I, and finally to that conference itself. In contrast to the developing countries' demand for the introduction of a generalised uniform system of preferences to apply to all imports of manufactures and semi-manufactures from developing to developed countries, the plan proposed the negotiation of 'selective, temporary and degressive' preferences, product by product, between interested exporting developing countries and importing developed countries.

The Belgian case for this plan was twofold. First, it could quickly create effective and workable machinery for negotiating preferences between developed and developing countries – in contrast to establishing a common list of generalised preferences for goods from all developing countries which, it was thought, would be at best slow in execution, and, at worst, impractical. Second, it would effectively limit the scope of preferences to those products which could be agreed in negotiation between individual developed countries (or groups such as the EEC) and individual developing countries (or, again, regional groupings). Preferential treatment was not to be envisaged for products in which ldcs were already fully competitive, or for those 'manufactured under abnormal economic conditions, and thus offered at prices appreciably below those of most domestic or foreign producers who are the habitual suppliers of the import market'.[2] In these cases (presumably such items as cotton textiles and jute products where Belgian industry had a particularly strong interest in maintaining protection) Brasseur proposed that, under international agreement, a compensatory tax, presumably raised from part or the whole of the import duty on such products, be given as aid to the exporting countries.

The Brasseur Plan was thus to use preferences only as a means of aiding *new* exports from developing countries to break into international markets, much as Prebisch had originally proposed. Brasseur argued that many products which could not be sold on the international market under competitive conditions could become competitive through 'appropriate measures and assistance',[3] and that tariff preferences would make a valuable contribution to expanding the market and opening it to competition. 'These preferences should be adapted to the needs of each particular case and to the conditions of the importing market. This could be achieved through negotiations between the parties concerned. The initiative would, of course, lie with the would-be exporting country.[4] In a further statement to the UNCTAD Committee, the Belgian ambassador (Mr P.A. Forthomme) clarified the type of bilateral negotiations foreseen. They would not be conducted to bring about concessions on both sides; no reciprocity would be involved, in keeping with the principle agreed by GATT. But they would cover three topics: whether the manufactures put up for preferential treatment had a 'reasonable' possibility of becoming competitive, whether a preference would be likely to create difficulties in the importing market, and what would be the most effective margins of preference and time scale for phasing out.

A paper prepared for UNCTAD I by the research department of the UN Economic and Social Council (ECOSOC)[5] brought out the main problem – the complexity – of a Brasseur-type preference scheme. It foresaw the fragmentation of world trade into 'literally scores' of new preferential regimes, and the possibility of serious conflicts of interest among developing countries treated in different ways by the same importing country. Furthermore, a situation might evolve of almost perpetual negotiations between individual developed and developing countries on individual products, in which the preference-granting countries could completely control the extension of trade concessions to their own advantage.

The ECOSOC secretariat was perhaps disingenuous, however, in some of its wider criticisms of the Brasseur proposals, many of which – for example, that 'the choice of industries by the developed countries to be favoured with preferential treatment might be strongly influenced by considerations of domestic competition'[6] or that 'there could be a tendency to exclude large sectors of industry on the grounds that these were already well established or that they could not be viable'[7] – might equally well have been levied against *any* preferential system aimed at promoting infant industries and were certainly taken into account by Prebisch. In fact these reflect many of the shortcomings of actual GSP schemes, which themselves show up the desire of all the Western governments involved in the exercise to safeguard the most sensitive sectors of their economies and to minimise and share the burden of preferential imports.

The presentation of the Brasseur plan at UNCTAD I met with little sympathy from the developing countries, which were firmly committed to the principle of generalised preferences for all manufactured and semi-manufactured products from all developing countries. In particular the idea that products in which ldcs could already compete on world markets should be excluded, and the implication that products which sold cheaply in western markets were the result of 'abnormal' economic conditions, were unacceptable. Politically, the scheme was seen as dividing the developing countries according to their interests in exporting particular products, with the possibility of playing countries or groups off against one another; or as a means of maintaining special trading advantages for particular groups such as the Yaoundé Associates. This was thoroughly out of tune with the atmosphere of UNCTAD I, at which the (possibly) tenuous solidarity of the developing countries as a group was being given its first test.

In any case, it was clear that there was no agreement among the Six themselves – far less other rich countries – on the Brasseur plan. For the EEC Commission Mr Rey expressed himself 'profoundly in sympathy'[8] with the plan; the French Finance Minister, Mr Giscard d'Estaing, was less enthusiastic, although he felt that 'no doubt we could make good use of the suggestions which were put forward so admirably by Mr Brasseur'.[9] His view was that a simple solution could be found to the problem of access for semi-finished and partly processed products in the form of reducing 'certain excessively high' tariffs. For manufactures, however, he stressed the difficulties of the situation:

> . . . 'it is true to say that the less developed countries are not in a position to compete normally, and consequently to develop their exports.
>
> A very large majority of them suffer simultaneously from the handicap of technical backwardness and inadequate financial means or commercial networks. Some products, on the other hand, benefit from exceptional advantages in some countries, which sooner or later inevitably leads to a defensive attitude on the part of the importing countries.'[10]

More positively, he suggested that developed countries should agree to a target regular increase, perhaps fixed as a percentage growth rate, for their imports of manufactures from developing countries.

The West German and Netherlands representatives (Ministers Schmucker and Andriessen) were quite plainly in line with the British position that generalised tariff preferences for ldcs should be an advance stage in the general reduction of tariffs looked for in the Kennedy Round. West Germany regarded the measure as a way of 'providing an additional impulse to the developing countries' exports of semi-finished and finished manufactures'[11] while the Dutch Minister saw it as a means of creating 'realistic opportunities for the outlet of industrial manufactures and semi-manufactures from the developing countries'.[12] The Italian government, however, was totally opposed to the idea of preferences for developing countries:

> 'as far as manufactures and finished goods are concerned, we must first rid ourselves of generalisations and exaggerations.
>
> In our view, it is only in exceptional cases that special measures are required to facilitate the access of existing products to our markets. The difficulties which arise are in fact more related to marketing methods and product quality. It is these difficulties which the developing countries must seek to overcome, if necessary, with our assistance, if they are to find new outlets on terms which will avoid recourse to the protectionist measures hitherto provoked by competition . . . In any event, we feel that it is only by analysing particular situations that we can gain an idea of the magnitude of those problems which may require appropriate temporary solutions.'[13]

The one point of unity among the Community countries at this stage was that four out of the five major members were, at least in principle, in favour of some kind of preferential trading access for products from developing countries. There was, very clearly, no agreement among the Six as to the form, scope or duration of such preferential trading access; nor, in effect, on the reasons for extending preferences to developing countries. Germany and the Netherlands, with a generally liberal attitude to world trade development, looked on preferential terms for ldcs as a stage in general freeing of trade; to them, access to the market was the most important point. *Preferential* access should fall off naturally as free trade was developed. Belgium and France, with an eye to the industrial pressures involved,[14] were in favour of a much more cautious approach. They saw preferences not as a stage in the development of a free-trading system, but rather as a special concession: a deviation from a normal level of tariff protection, to be re-imposed as and when ldcs became competitive producers of manufactures.

It was clear from the debates held in the Committee on Manufactures at UNCTAD I that there was no hope of an agreement on a preferential tariff system for ldcs. Against a group of developing countries which were well co-ordinated and, at this stage, firmly behind a wide-ranging demand for preferential access for the vast majority of products, there was a very wide range of policies and attitudes among the rich countries, from outright opposition to any deviation from non-discriminatory mfn tariffs by the USA to active support for 'advance' tariff reductions for ldcs (if all developed countries took part) by Britain, the Netherlands and West Germany. The discussion was referred back to a Special Committee on Preferences, set up by the Secretary General of the United Nations,[15] charged with 'working out the best method of implementing such preferences on the basis of non-reciprocity from the developing countries, as well as to discuss further . . . differences of principle'.[16] This committee met only once, in June 1965.

The First Special Committee

From the start, the developing countries kept up a steady pressure on the developed members of the Committee. The principal position paper, submitted by nine developing countries,[17] made the following main demands:

1. Developed countries should extend tariff preferences to all manufactures and semi-manufactures imported from all ldcs, in two steps:
   (a) a total immediate elimination of tariffs on products of cottage industries and handmade goods processed from materials produced in ldcs and goods on which the normal mfn duty rate was 10 per cent or less;
   (b) an immediate 50 per cent reduction in mfn duties on all other manufactured and semi-manufactured goods produced in ldcs, with

a view to total elimination of import duties over five years. The preferences would last for at least ten years, after which they would be reviewed by an 'appropriate international body' nominated by UNCTAD.

2. Exceptions might be justified on 'grounds of overriding national economic interest' and should be subject to international consultation. Similarly, preferences could be suspended if preferential imports were shown to be dislocating the market in a particular importing country.

3. No new quota restrictions should be introduced which could'nullify or impair' the effects of preferences; and existing quota restrictions should be eliminated.

4. Provision for preferential entry for manufactures and semi-manufactures from developing countries should be written into the rules of international trade.

Against these points, the major developed countries represented in the Special Committee had few new proposals. The United States was still determinedly opposed to preferences in principle;[18] the United Kingdom rested on its position that it would be prepared to cut tariffs on manufactures and semi-manufactures imported from ldcs if all developed countries did so together, on condition that Commonwealth developing countries should waive their rights to guaranteed margins of preference on particular products, and so long as GSP tariff cuts did not hold back the general reduction of mfn rates. In particular the UK delegation declared itself strongly opposed to the selectivity of the Brasseur plan:

> 'It seems reasonably plain that all developing countries need to export more and to earn more foreign exchange and that any reduction in tariff barriers, whether preferential or not, will help them to it . . . We believe, therefore, that any principle of selection of countries on the basis of need for preferences should be rejected. We think it would be invidious to put developing countries in the position of applicants, as it were, for piecemeal preferential tariff concessions'.[19]

France, in turn, was still strongly opposed to a general and universal system of preferential access which would apply equally to all developing countries, and in favour of the selective Brasseur approach. Preferences 'should not be general'[20] because some products were already fully competitive, while others would be subject to reservations or safeguards in importing countries (and each importing country's list would be different), and because not all ldcs – particularly, not those which were mainly primary commodity exporters – could benefit. Universal preferences applied equally to all ldcs, moreover, would in fact discriminate in favour of those which were more competitive or developed from the outset; and if preferences were to be neither general nor universal, the French delegation argued, only through negotiations between importing and exporting countries could lists and terms be drawn up. Developing countries which could make some type of reciprocal gesture – which might be, for example, a commitment to taking part in 'the possibilities of regional integration'[21] – should do so, while the possibility of extending 'broader preferences to the most disadvantaged countries'[22] should be kept open.

By contrast, the German delegation favoured a general approach. All, or at least the major, developed countries were 'to grant all developing countries substantial tariff preferences for semi-manufactured and manufactured goods of special export interest to developing countries on a non-discriminatory basis and without reciprocal tariff concessions.'[23] Such preferences were to be negotiated in the GATT 'as a concerted action of the developed countries' on the basis of a positive list agreed between the developed and developing countries involved. The list would be in two parts: the first 'as large as possible' in which all products would be given preferential treatment by all developed countries; and a second, from which each developed country might exclude 'a certain percentage' of goods. Preferential treatment would last for a fixed period of, say, ten years during which the margin of preference would be progressively reduced either by raising to the mfn rates once again or by lowering the latter to the preferential level. The list of products on which preferences were granted would be reviewed periodically. Developed countries would have the right to suspend preferences temporarily, if market disruption could be shown, after bilateral consultations with the developing countries concerned.

Thus, three distinctly different points of view were at this stage apparent among developed countries. The USA, backed by Canada, Switzerland and Japan, and to a lesser extent by Sweden and Norway, was against the idea of preferences in principle.[24] The United Kingdom, Germany and the Netherlands were broadly in favour of liberal preferential access for developing countries' exports as a way of giving ldcs an 'advance' on the major trade liberalisation measures which, it was still hoped, would result from the Kennedy Round, while France and Italy approved the selective approach taken by Belgium in the Brasseur plan. The conflict of views apparent among Community members over the subject was largely resolved during the next two years, during the work of the UNCTAD Group on Preferences and the OECD Special Group on Trade with Developing Countries.

Institutional Links: EEC/OECD/UNCTAD

All the member states of the Community are also members of OECD, as they are of the B Group[25] in UNCTAD. Since the inception of UNCTAD, the OECD has acted as a co-ordinating agency and a forum for discussion of general policy lines among the B Group. Gosović notes that

> 'Within the OECD, a decision on the general policy line is taken; it is on the basis of this decision that the B Group in UNCTAD adjusts its position to the dynamic elements that arise. The static context in the OECD and the absence of the other negotiating party usually necessitate a departure from the original position. However . . . when an important issue is involved, and when the position reached in the OECD is in the form of a package deal among the developed countries, the changes can only be nominal or tactical in nature'.[26]

This is not to say that the developed Western countries necessarily agree on every detail of all policy questions likely to be raised in an UNCTAD forum. Nor is it to suggest that differences are necessarily swept under the carpet in secret OECD discussion in the interests of holding a 'line'. But it is clear that Western countries, including those of the Community, do attach great importance to OECD discussions, and coordinate their OECD and UNCTAD representation to the extent that the members of B Group delegations in UNCTAD are often also the members of the most relevant OECD Committees or working parties.[27] It has become normal for B Group Representatives to meet in Paris to discuss UNCTAD issues before any meetings.

For EEC countries, there are then three levels at which discussion of UNCTAD questions takes place; in the EEC Council of Ministers and its subsidiary bodies, in OECD, and in UNCTAD and its subsidiary committees. The EEC Commission participates in all three alongside the member states. Its status in UNCTAD is that of an intergovernmental observer, and while not a contracting party to the OECD Convention it takes part in the OECD's work under Protocol 1 to the Convention. During 1966 and 1967 work on the question of extending generalised preferences was concentrated in OECD and the UNCTAD Group on Preferences. Although EEC member states, increasingly prompted and co-ordinated by the work of the Commission, moved towards a common attitude during this period, there was not yet a 'Community' policy on the subject, and the member states (France and Germany in particular) substantially made the running as far as the EEC was concerned.

The OECD Special Group Report: a crucial declaration

Initially, OECD co-ordination on the GSP took place in the Working Party of the Trade Committee. But the most important work to define a common position for the Western countries as a whole was done by the Special Group on Trade with Developing Countries (the 'Four Wise Men') set up by the OECD Council at its meeting in November 1965. It consisted of four senior trade officials of the United Kingdom, the USA, France and West Germany, appointed as national representatives working to define a common line which could be pursued with OECD Ministers. The brief given to the group was to 'undertake an examination of the problems regarding trade between developed and developing countries with a view to formulating constructive and concerted policies':[29] a broad formula, but one which was necessary to permit the USA, at that stage still opposed in principle to the idea of special tariff treatment for ldcs, to take part in the Group.

The OECD Group held two working sessions: from 26 July to 5 August 1966 and from 4 to 18 July 1967. It submitted an interim report to the November 1966 meeting of the OECD Council; and its final report to the Council meeting on 1 December 1967 was forwarded to UNCTAD in January 1968.[30] Because of the radical differences of principle between the attitudes of the USA and all the other members of the group all discussion of the preference issue was completely deadlocked until after the Declaration of Punta del Este made by President Johnson in April 1967, expressing the United States' readiness to extend preferential treatment to Latin America. Then things began to move ahead:

> 'The Group have concentrated their attention on the question "how" rather than "whether" to grant special tariff treatment. They are agreed that the concession of special tariff treatment in developed country markets could help the developing countries to increase their export earnings.'[31]

The report of the Group forms the core of the OECD 'donor' countries' ideas on generalised preferences or, as the report put it, 'special tariff treatment for developing countries'.[32] The three basic principles on which the group were able to agree have become the basis of all the GSP schemes so far introduced, and remained unaltered since the publication of the report. The principles were:
(a) that the concession of special tariff treatment in developed country markets could help the developing countries to increase their export earnings, and that any such arrangements should not imply any reciprocal advantages for developed countries' exports in ldc markets';[33]

(b) that special tariff treatment should in principle apply to all products in chapters 25-99 of the Brussels tariff nomenclature (BTN) – which the group defined arbitrarily as 'manufactured and semi-manufactured products' – while other products could be included on a case-by-case basis;[34]
(c) that any country claiming ldc status should be accepted as eligible in principle for special treatment under the scheme.

The OECD Group also concluded that, although any special tariff treatment extended to ldcs should not be allowed to stand in the way of future reductions in most favoured nation tariffs, it must be granted for an initial period of ten years.[35] But there was no agreement between the members of the group on whether duty-free access should be the rule or, if not, what depth of tariff reduction should be given:[36] what kinds of safeguard procedures should be recommended in cases of 'market disruption' (although the Group were agreed that some safeguards should be built into the system);[37] a common set of criteria for deciding on exceptions to GSP lists (although it was thought probable that developed countries would wish to exclude 'a limited number of products in respect of which developing countries are already competitive').[38] The Group's failure to agree on safeguards and exceptions reflected the differences between the 'escape clause' GSP system with no *a priori* restrictions as introduced by Britain and the Scandinavian countries, and the 'tariff quota' system as introduced by the EEC and Japan.

Parallel work in UNCTAD: the Group on Preferences

The work of the UNCTAD Group on Preferences ran very closely parallel to that of the OECD's 'Four Wise Men'. It was through this group that UNCTAD provided the main impetus for bringing the views of developing and developed countries together and the developing countries attempted to persuade the developed world to take as liberal as possible an attitude to the GSP. The Group, like the OECD group, held two main sessions, from 16 July to 5 August 1966 and from 4 to 18 July 1967; and once again the latter session, after the Punta del Este declaration, was the more productive of the two. Again, the principal questions which concerned the Group related to the range of products which preference schemes should include; the countries which should be eligible; the length of time for which preference schemes should last (in particular, whether preferential access would last long enough to allow export-oriented industries to be established); whether objective criteria could be developed for the application of safeguards and escape clauses, given that developed countries were likely to take action to protect 'sensitive' industries; whether special measures could, or should, be taken to promote exports from the least advanced developing countries; and how Commonwealth and Yaoundé preferences could be reconciled with the GSP.

Since France and West Germany were the only two EEC member states represented on both the UNCTAD and the OECD groups, it is not very surprising that their views played an important part in the discussions and carried over into the EEC's own debates on the GSP. Moreover, just as it was in this period that the general lines of the GSP schemes introduced in the end were roughed out, it is evident from the UNCTAD discussion that during this time French and German views moved very much closer together. On the one hand, France abandoned its advocacy of the Brasseur plan, in the face of the wide-ranging objections by all ldcs and the majority of developed 'donor' countries to the selective, negotiated nature of the scheme; on the other, German representatives, who had always advocated the introduction of a GSP in principle;[39] defined their attitudes to the operation of a system more closely. In particular the French and German representatives agreed, in the second session of the Group, that a system involving some form of tariff quota as a safeguard against 'market disruption' would be preferable, as far as they were concerned, to one involving an escape clause under which tariffs suspended under GSP could be reintroduced at will by a donor country.

There is little doubt that two particular aspects of the 'safeguards' question influenced both French and German viewpoints strongly. First, a tariff quota system providing for a ceiling level of duty-free imports (however the ceiling was defined) would give the importing country greater control over the volume of preferential imports entering than any 'escape clause could. It was argued that a tariff quota system (as the UNCTAD secretariat had pointed out in its discussion document for the Group[40]), 'constituted a guarantee for the developing countries that preferential imports from them could not suddenly be stopped for alleged market disruption; thus enabling those countries to plan better their exports to the industrialised countries'.[41] Second, a tariff quota system could ensure that the 'burden' of preferential imports was equitably 'shared' among developed countries; everyone could see in advance how far each donor country was prepared to go in letting in preferential imports. The French representative argued – significantly – that 'the automatic quota system protected not the country applying the preferences but the countries benefiting from them since it spared them from cut-throat competition, which, by lowering prices, caused them to lose the advantage of the preferences they had been granted'.[42] For France, clearly the GSP was more a means of ensuring the profitability of ldc exports than of increasing their access to Western

markets.
Two further points may be added. A tariff quota system in the GSP context was consistent both with arrangements being operated by individual EEC members (France, Germany, Benelux) in bilateral agreements, and with new Community tariff quota provisions to be introduced in 1968.[43] In this sense it could be said to be more *communautaire* than a simple escape clause. The EEC Commission has argued strongly, too, that an escape clause system in a Community of six members, each with their own industries to protect, would be unworkable because of the large possible number of applications and demands for safeguard provisions.

It was clearly important for Community countries as well as for the EEC Commission that differences of view between the members on the subject of GSP should be reconciled in order to create a common policy. And the evolution of a consensus both reveals the working of EEC decision making on question of external affairs, illustrating the relations between the member states, the Commission, and 'outsiders', and indicates how the process of debate and reconciliation within the Community – which does not necessarily take place *inside* Community institutions – itself influences the interests of the countries affected by these policies. In this case, two of the three countries with the largest voting rights on the Council of Ministers had by 1967 reached an important measure of agreement on the principle of generalised preferences, and on one major element in the type of scheme which would be introduced. At this stage, there had been no formal discussion of the GSP question by the EEC Council of Ministers as such, although a position paper setting out the general issues had been prepared by the Commission in November 1966; and most of the discussion of GSP issues had taken place in international non-Community organisations. However, the development of Franco-German agreement on these basic principles – although not on the detailed machinery of a scheme) was a strong influence on the work undertaken by the EEC Commission departments from late 1966 onwards.

NOTES

1 *Conclusions and Resolutions adopted at the GATT Ministerial Meeting on 21 May 1963.*
2 Statement by H.E. Mr. Maurice Brasseur (Belgium). UNCTAD 1. Proceedings. Vol.II, pp. 108-13.
3. *Ibid.*
4 *Ibid.*
5 'Trade in Manufactures and Semi-manufactures', UNCTAD I, *Proceedings,* Vol.IV, pp. 3-4

6 *Ibid.*, para 143
7 *Ibid.*
8 Statement by M. Jean Rey (EEC Commission) UNCTAD I, *Proceedings*, Vol.II, p. 445
9 Statement by H.E. Mr. Valéry Giscard d'Estaing (France), *op.cit.* p. 197.
10 *Ibid.*
11 Statement by H.E. Mr. Kurt Schmucker (West Germany), *op.cit.* p. 191
12 Statement by H.E. Mr. J.E. Andriessen (Netherlands), *op.cit.* p. 289.
13 Statement by H.E. Mr. Bernardo Mattarella (Italy), *op.cit.* p.238.
14 In particular the Brasseur plan's proposal for compensatory aid from import duty on low-priced products is very similar to an idea put forward by the Federation of Belgian Industries (F.I.B.) in 1968.
15 The Committee had to be established in this way since UNCTAD itself was not, at that stage, a permanent UN agency, and had no permanent secretariat.
16 UNCTAD I, Resolution A.III.5 *Proceedings*, Vol.I, p. 39.
17 Argentina, Brazil, India, Nigeria, Pakistan, Philippines, Senegal, United Arab Republic and Yugoslavia.
18 TD/B/C.2/1 Add.1, Annex B, p.26. The US, however, did propose that other 'promising measures' be pursued, such as mfn duty reductions on products of special interest to ldcs, assistance in marketing ldc products in Western and developing countries, and the strengthening of commodity markets.
19 *Op.cit.*, p. 76.
20 *Op.cit.*, p. 41.
21 *Op.cit.*, p. 42
22 *Ibid.*
23 *Op.cit.*, p. 79
24 See Branislav Gosović, *UNCTAD: Conflict and Compromise*, A.W. Sijthoff, Leiden, 1972, p. 70.
25 Gosović,*op.cit.*, p. 46. The B Group comprises 29 countries. Of these 20 are characterised by Gosović as being 'serious candidates' for the 18 seats on the UNCTAD Trade and Development Board allotted to the B Group. 11 of these – the USA, Belgium, West Germany, France, Italy, the Netherlands, Switzerland, the UK, Japan, Canada and Australia, effectively have permanent seats on the Board. These countries are all OECD members.
26 *Ibid.*, p. 294.
27 The most relevant committee in this case was the Trade Committee. Most of the co-ordinating work among the OECD members is done in the Working Party set up by this Committee, whose membership (of officials) can be tailored to the subject to be discussed and which can meet as and when required (the full Committee meets only twice a year).
28 The British representative was Mr Sidney Golt of the Board of Trade
29 Statement by the OECD Ministerial Council, *OECD Observer*, December 1965.
30 Published as TD/56, 29 January 1968.
31 *Ibid.*, Part Two, para 4.
32 The phrase 'special tariff treatment' was deliberate. As Jean Scheurer, Head of Division in the Trade Department of OECD, indicates: *OECD Observer*, February 1968, p. 6: 'In the past the term "preferences" was used to designate arrangements applied among restricted groups of countries, developed or not, and therefore involving discrimination in respect of all countries outside the groups in question. By using the expression "special tariff treatment" it was hoped to avoid the idea of some countries being given an advantage over others, and suggest in its place a system which would not apply to groups of selected countries but to a whole category of countries characterised by their less-developed state. With this new concept of a special trade policy applying

to all developing countries, action by the developed countries would no longer add to the number and diversity of existing trade systems, but on the contrary tend to reduce them by gradually overlaying the present compartmentalisation of the world with a simpler system more in keeping with the principle of non-discrimination, whereby all the developing countries would in the last analysis be placed on an equal footing as regards the sale of their manufactures to the developed countries'.

33 TD/56, Annex, Part One. J: and Part Two, para 4.

34 *Ibid.*, Part One, B: and Part Two paras 16 and 17. The US representative was the sole dissenter, insisting that *all* products subject to import duties in developed countries should be included in principle.

35 *Ibid.*, Part One, E: and Part Two, para. 37.

36 *Ibid.*, Part One, F: and Part Two, para. 26.

37 *Ibid.*, Part One, G: and Part Two, paras. 27-33.

38 *Ibid.*, Part One, C: and Part Two, paras. 18-21.

39 See above, p. 42.

40 TD/B/C.2/AC.1/7, *The Question of granting an extension of preferences in favour of developing countries.*

41 TD/B/C.2/AC.1/SR.15. Summary record of the 15th meeting of the Group. p. 4 and 5.

42 *Ibid.*, p. 9.

43 France, Germany and Italy had four Council votes each: Belgium and the Netherlands two: and Luxembourg one. (R. Mayne, *The Institutions of the European Community,* Chatham House/PEP, 1968, p.18).

6. HISTORY OF THE COMMUNITY GSP: THE DEVELOPMENT OF A COMMON POLICY

Joint responsibility for tariff questions is fundamental to the EEC, under Chapter 1 of the Treaty of Rome. Responsibility for administering the Common External Tariff and for conducting tariff negotiations is placed on the Commission, and that for changing the level of tariffs on the Council. A question such as the extension of generalised preferences is thus clearly one which concerns the Community as a whole.

It was noted above[1] that it was the EEC as a negotiating entity, led by Mr. Jean Rey, then Commissioner for External Relations, which was represented in the original GATT working party on preferences in 1963. Mr Rey's open advocacy of the Brasseur plan, however, was not supported by all the member states; while in line with the views of the Belgian and French governments at the time, it did not square with those of Germany and the Netherlands, which favoured the generalised approach.

This division was reflected in the member states' approach to UNCTAD I and in the OECD and UNCTAD discussions on preferences which followed the conference, where the Community as a body did not take part. It was not until November 1966 that a Commission again attempted openly to promote a Community policy on preferences.

There were several reasons for this hesitation. Preferences were, at the time, rather a side-issue for developed countries, despite the attempts by the ldcs in UNCTAD and in the First Special Committee to make them central. The developed countries could not at the start agree even on the principle of preferences. The Kennedy Round was their main preoccupation, and one which took a substantial proportion of officials' negotiating skills. Lastly, during the period from June 1965 to February 1966 Community institutions themselves were caught up in the crisis created by France's virtual boycott of the Community.[2]

There can be little doubt that, after this crisis, the Commission was much more cautious in making and pursuing new policy initiatives. This caution is borne out in the way GSP policy was developed by the Commission. In theory this was an ideal policy for the Commission to work on. It was relatively technical and bureaucratic in nature: it was one where all the member states except Italy were agreed (at least in broadest principle) and it was one where it seemed, given ldcs clear desire for preferential access to Western markets, that the Community action could enhance its reputation with developing countries as an outward-looking, liberal-minded trading entity. Moreover, success in promoting a 'European' policy on GSP would in itself strengthen the influence of the Commission in the Community and expand the area in which Community policy governed the individual actions of member states.

But in practice, the Commission was required to build on a partly completed framework of ideas and agreements on how a system of preferences should be establsihed, and to parallel, in its own work, the independent decision-making processes of the OECD and UNCTAD committees where the Western countries' policies were being hammered out. By 1966 attitudes to GSP were becoming fairly well defined, at least in principle. One of the strongest elements in Western attitudes to a scheme was the desire to share the 'burden' of imports at preferential rates among importing countries. This requirement inhibited the rapid development of a system of preferences internationally, particularly as long as the attitude of the USA remained in doubt. Within the Community, too, when it came to questions of detail, internal burden-sharing requirements among the Six created the most serious limitations on the scope of the system.

However the Commission was able to trade on the need for the question to be settled at Community level (since it touched on the Common External Tariff) and the measure of basic agreement which existed among all member states except Italy. Nevertheless, despite the Commission's caution and its careful attempt to assess what preferential concessions the member states would accept, the combination of national protectionism with the idea of burden-sharing among the Six determined that the value of the scheme to ldcs would be relatively small.

The Commission's Role

The 1966-67 period marked a watershed in international debate on the GSP. The report of the 'Four Wise Men' to OECD had largely settled the basic issue of whether developed countries should introduce preference schemes and had put forward a set of ground rules on which such schemes might be based. These were to be strongly challenged, but without a great deal of success, by the developing countries at and after UNCTAD II in New Delhi; and from then on, both within the Community and at the international level, the details of the 'offers' to be made by developed countries were the main subject of debate and controversy.

This watershed is reflected in the Commission's work. After the initial unsuccessful attempt to promote the Brasseur plan Commission officials, though active, operated mainly in the background. Their aim was to hold the ring for the member states, to promote agreement between them (particularly to bring together pro-Brasseur and anti-Brasseur elements, if possible) and to follow the discussions in OECD and UNCTAD, in order to ensure that the Six went into UNCTAD II at least broadly agreed on the principles of a GSP scheme. The Commission did not, and could not, attempt to impose a point of view on the member states: the aim was, rather, to build on their attitudes to the development of the GSP, to reach a 'European' policy.[3]

Although any memorandum from the Commission to the Council is voted on by, and submitted in the name of, the whole Commission, proposals originate within particular departments (Directorates-General) with particular officials or groups of officials working with the support of the Commissioner at the head of the particular department. It is obvious that different departments, or even different divisions and sections within one department, will have different policy interests to defend, more or less strongly depending on their importance in 'Community' policy. Where a particular policy proposal cuts across the interests of more than one department, bargains and alliances must be struck up, if the measure concerned is likely to be controversial.

Occasionally, where international negotiation is undertaken by the Commission on behalf of the Community, as in the Kennedy Round or the enlargement negotiations, these alliances may be formalised into a negotiating team which can act more or less independently of departmental preoccupations. Such major negotiations would probably be the only occasions when special teams of this type would be established; in the GSP, although quite a wide range of Community interests was affected, this was not necessary. But a definite pattern of alliance for and against, within Commission departments, became clear, and the first problem for the GSP scheme's designers was to create something which could in itself satisfy the differing interests within the Commission.

The department with direct responsibility for the GSP was, and remains, DG I, the Directorate General for External Affairs. Initially this was headed by Commissioner Edoardo Martino: latterly, from 1970 onwards, by Ralf Dahrendorf. Within the department, GSP work was carried out by the Division for UNCTAD and General Affairs, headed by Mattia di Martino. He and his deputy and successor Tran Van-Thinh became most closely identified with the GSP among Commission officials: indeed, the scheme is largely regarded as their personal brain-child. Although DGI was primarily responsible for the GSP, however, cooperation with DG VIII (Development Co-operation) was close: many of the Commission working documents on the proposals were issued in the joint names of Martino, Jean-François Deniau (before 1970, responsible for External Trade, latterly, responsible for DG VIII) and

Henri Rochereau, the Commissioner for Development Aid up to 1970. While such top-level support was no doubt essential for DG I efforts in this area to succeed, it also ensured that the GSP would conflict as little as possible with the prior claims of Association.

Commission work before UNCTAD II

The Commission's first priority in the period leading up to the New Delhi UNCTAD conference was to persuade the Six that they should work out a common attitude to the GSP. Its initial arguments were based on the high political value set by developing countries on the GSP as a means of helping the start of industrialisation, contrasted with the small degree of disruption to Community economies likely to result from tariff cuts on ldcs manufactures – the Common External Tariff being already relatively low for most manufactured goods. Even assuming duty-free treatment as the rule – not yet settled – the price advantage which preferences would give ldcs would be relatively small; and price advantage was only one element, not necessarily the most important, in gaining a trade advantage in manufactures.

Because of this, the Commission argued, it should be relatively easy for the Community to agree on a scheme. The most important features of the Community preference scheme should be (1) simplicity (in particular, freedom from customs and administrative complications) and (2) compatibility with the maintenance of the general multilateral system of world trade relations. Special tariff treatment should be temporary, and legalized either by a waiver or by an amendment to GATT rules; but in order to be of any value to developing countries, it should last long enough, and provide a margin of preference wide enough to stimulate the export from ldcs of new products, or products which, though not yet competitive on world markets, had an opportunity under preferential incentives of becoming so. Ten years' duration was suggested.

The idea that preferences should aim at stimulating the growth of 'new' export products recalls directly both the selective ideas of the Brasseur plan and the main argument advanced by Prebisch based on 'infant industry' promotion and expounded by the French delegation to the UNCTAD Group on Preferences. Also in line with French views (and with existing EEC policy) was a proviso that, in constructing a system of generalised preferences, the Community should not take on any commitments which would change the basis of its Association policy, without being completely assured that a world-wide GSP would adequately replace the benefits which Associates gained from preferential access to the European market by extending 'equivalent concessions' in other markets. This point, on which the Associates were very insistent in UNCTAD II, was a major block to the extension of GSP on processed agricultural products.[4]

Although the main tenor of the Commission's argument was that a GSP would have relatively little effect, it was foreseen that if, as was likely, the initial benefits of preferential access on manufactures went to the countries with the most highly developed manufacturing industries and if those manufacturing industries were directly competitive with vulnerable sectors of the EEC economy, safeguards could be applied. The Commission suggested that duty-free access could be limited by a combination of a general safeguard clause and specific tariff quotas. The latter could be used where duty-free access was extended; a general safeguard clause where only partial reductions in duty were envisaged (which corresponds preeisely with what happened in the end). But the Commission recommended that the use of tariff quotas should be kept to a minimum, because of the administrative complications.

The Commission proposed that the Community authorities draw up positive lists of products where preferences might be extended, as a starting point for consultations with ldcs. In this way a product-by-product solution to the question could be worked out. It was also suggested that there might be some practical advantage in consulting with groups of ldcs interested in particular products or ranges of products, as well as with *all* ldcs on the general principles of the scheme.

The system proposed by the Commission was thus a curious mixture of Brasseur plan and UNCTAD proposals. But even at this stage many of the features which eventually became part of the Community GSP were already evident. Although neither product nor country coverage were settled – as, indeed, they had not been in the OECD discussions – the possibility of a conflict between the special preferences enjoyed by Associates and the creation of a GSP, the use of tariff quotas on sensitive products, and the ten-year duration of GSP later adopted internationally, were, at least in outline, established.

These principles were carried forward into the Commission's comments on the report of the OECD Special Group. Broadly, the Commission recommended Community endorsement of the Four Wise Men's report, but had reservations on two points:

(1) Any attempt to harmonise preference schemes in order to share the 'burden' of imports should not be so rigid as to hold up indefinitely the introduction of GSP schemes:

(2) Preferences for processed agricultural products governed by Common Market regulations should not exceed the 'industrial protection' element of the import duty.[5] Where products were subject both to CAP variable levies and flat rate import duties, only the flat rate tariff could be considered for preferential cuts. No reductions in CAP

levies could be granted: a provision which would maintain both protection for European farmers and privileges for Yaoundé Associates, which did benefit from selective CAP levy reductions.

The Commission's major objection was, not unnaturally, to the US representative's view that the abolition of 'reverse' preferences given by Associates to Community exports was a precondition of establishing a GSP. The defence (or attack) on this view became a classic of its type. The 'free-trade area' under which the Community gave preferential access to goods from Associates and some Associates gave preferences to some Community exports was, it was argued, legally necessary to conform with GATT rules. Moreover, Associates (being principally exporters of agricultural and mineral products and of processed agricultural goods) would not benefit from the extension of a generalised system of preferences on manufactures. If reverse preferences were abandoned then the Community's preferences for AASM products were also called into question. So if the creation of a GSP required the abandonment of reverse preferences (and the possibility that EEC preferences would be abandoned) not only would the AASM fail to benefit from GSP, but their interests would be directly harmed.[6]

The Commission's views on preferences changed only a little following the OECD report. Its briefing memorandum to the Council of Ministers before UNCTAD II[7] (which was never actually considered by the full Council, but by COREPER) made the following points:

(1) The Community should approve the principle of generalised preferences.

(2) It should consider excluding some products entirely from preferential treatment (if ldcs were considered completely competitive in these fields). Sensitive products (such as cotton textiles, clothing, photographic equipment, radios, sewing machines) would be subject to tariff quotas which would prevent damage to domestic industries.

(3) It should consider ruling out certain countries for products in which these were particularly competitive (a point which runs directly counter to the ideas expressed by the OECD Group).[8]

(4) Sensitive products' access could alternatively be limited by granting only partial reductions in duty to these goods. Tariff quotas, it was recognised, would create administrative difficulties. For non-sensitive products, all mfn duties under 10 per cent should be eliminated and 'substantial' cuts made in higher rates.

(5) For competing processed agricultural goods (pags) a limited preferential cut in the industrial processing element of the tariff might be considered, but no cuts in CAP levies.

(6) Non-competing pags should be included in the scheme subject to consultation with Associates; 'special' or 'additional' preferences might be envisaged linked to the development of new processing or

industrialisation projects, especially those financed by aid. (This last is once again a derivative of the Brasseur plan.)

Although the Commission adopted the broad view that processed agricultural products should be included, it is clear that it stood by the OECD Group's position that they be assessed 'case by case'. This position was not one the developing countries were prepared to accept without a fight; and the fight was carried forward into the Second Committee of UNCTAD II, where proposals put up by the developing countries of the Group of 77 refer consistently to 'manufactures, including processed and semi-processed primary products'.

The conflict over product coverage was not soluble at UNCTAD II, and the developing countries had to accept that the West was not prepared to consider processed agricultural goods in the same way as 'manufactures', strictly defined, and that the best they could hope for would be a liberal set of 'positive lists' of processed products.[9] This affected many developing countries' attitudes to the GSP. In particular, it affected those held by the AASM Associates. *Agence Europe* noted, as UNCTAD II was starting,

> 'It is clear that the Associates could never give up a system which suits their purpose so admirably (the Yaoundé Convention) for a system which they know will not be to their advantage for a very long time, for the simple reason that manufactures only represent a small percentage of their exports. Their position will no doubt be supported by all the Common Market countries, despite the role that the Yaoundé Convention might play in internal Community negotiations.'[10]

In international discussions, and in public, the Community and its members were likely to support attitudes taken by the Yaoundé Associates to such subjects as the GSP, and defend any of their interests. But in this case the Associates' interests in minimising GSP access for processed agricultural goods coincided fairly closely with industrial interests in the EEC itself; and, moreover, international reluctance to admit processed goods under the GSP may in turn have strengthened the Associates' resolve to maintain any discriminatory benefits available under Association against erosion from wider ldc tariff cuts.

Settling the detail: Commission work after UNCTAD II

UNCTAD II produced no new agreement on the basis on which a GSP should be founded. Despite the last minute discussion and bargaining of an *ad hoc* contact group set up by the Secretary-General, the best that could be agreed in the final resolution[11] was to establish a further Special Committee on Preferences which should aim to 'settle the details of the arrangements in the course of 1969'.

For the OECD countries, the aim was to negotiate among themselves, on the basis of the Four Wise Men's report, on questions such as product coverage, safeguard clauses, rules of origin and procedures for consultation with developing countries on the use of safeguards. To this end, the OECD established in May 1968 an *ad hoc* working group of all the member countries which were intending to extend preferences to ldcs in which the EEC Commission took part alongside the Six. This group agreed that its members should prepare 'negative' lists of products in BTN chapters 25-99 ('manufactures') on which preferential treatment would *not* be given, and 'positive' lists of processed agricultural products in BTN chapters 1-24 on which preferential treatment *would* be given. The governments concerned were to submit their lists to the OECD by 1 March 1969. These would then be sent on for wider discussion with the developing countries in the UNCTAD Special Committee on Preferences.

Within the Community, the Council's Group on Trade Questions (an official sub-committee of the Committee of Permanent Representatives) discussed the GSP several times between March and November 1968. Unable to agree on any major points, the Group asked the Commission to prepare two particular lists of products; first, a list of the manufactures and semi-finished goods in BTN chapters 25-99 which could be regarded as 'sensitive' by Community interests, and, second, preliminary ideas on the processed agricultural goods which might be included in an EEC scheme. A working document prepared under the auspices of the three Commissioners most closely concerned[12] was sent to the Council on 15 November; it was discussed by the Group on Trade Questions in its December 1968 and January 1969 meetings. By the end of the set of discussions, the system which the EEC would introduce was well enough defined to meet the OECD March deadline.

Manufactures

The criteria on which a draft list of 'sensitive' manufactures had been prepared were as follows:

1. Hong Kong should not be given GSP access. (If Hong Kong had been included, it was argued, a much larger 'sensitive' list would be necessary.)
2. The rule for all non-sensitive products should be duty-free access.
3. Preferences on sensitive products should be limited either by tariff quotas *or* by only partial tariff cuts on these goods. (The Commission position on tariff quotas seems to have weakened by this stage, since

its earlier statements had warned against their use.'
4. A general safeguard clause should, in addition, be applied to both sensitive and non-sensitive products.

It was at this stage that the system to be applied to manufactures was settled. Duty-free treatment within tariff quotas (defined as outlined in Chapter 2 above) would in principle be applied to all imports of manufactures from ldcs, but in practice only to sensitive products, duty-free access for which would be suspended for the rest of the year in question when a ceiling was reached. Imports of other products could in practice exceed the ceilings; but if a complaint of 'market disruption' against a non-sensitive good was proved justified by the Commission, the product would be treated as sensitive in the following year. A supervisory mechanism based either on advance notice of import or on automatic licences would be installed for products regarded as potentially 'sensitive'.

The formula for tariff quotas appears to have been chosen completely arbitrarily, although it had earlier been decided to relate it to actual imports in some way. Publicly, the formula was justified as being 'a guarantee as to the amount of preferential imports that could be made'.[13] The EEC representative in the Special Committee on Preferences throught the initial ceilings 'would be fully sufficient to meet the needs of the developing countries'.

Processed Agricultural Goods

In contrast to their acceptance of Commission proposals on manufactures the processed agricultural goods list was heavily cut back by the Council experts to eliminate virtually any processed product about which any member state (but particularly France and Italy) felt sensitive. The Commission had proposed that all cereal flours and meals, a wide range of frozen, dried, or canned fruit and vegetables (including dried onions, frozen strawberries, canned tomatoes, olives, peaches and apricots, and canned fruit in general), and such items as coffee extracts, roast chicory and canned fish should be given at least a measure of GSP treatment. Many of these are products which were, or have since become, controlled under the CAP. None of these appeared in the final form of the scheme. The list which resulted from the Council's pruning was regarded by the Commission as the absolute minimum which could seriously be offered to UNCTAD. Any further reductions would, they thought, have made the scheme completely meaningless for ldcs interested in the processed farm and fishery products.

The Council accepted the Commission's proposals on the margin of preference – which were extremely limited. A margin equal to 50 per cent of the part of the tariff estimated to protect processing industry was taken as the general rule for 'normal' products. The 'processing element' itself was arbitrarily assessed at 40 per cent of the total mfn customs duty. Thus, for 'normal' products a GSP tariff cut of 20 per cent could be expected; for 'sensitive' products, a cut of 10 per cent. This level of tariff cuts appears to have been settled politically – on an intuitive assessment of what member states' governments, with their own 'constituencies' and domestic pressures, were prepared to countenance. Certainly, there is little or no economic rationale behind the arbitrary division of customs tariffs into a 'primary product' component of 60 per cent of the duty and an 'industrial processing' component of 40 per cent. Strictly speaking, it is the difference between the duty charged on a raw product and that on a processed good which represents (in nominal terms) the protection given to the processing industry. This obviously varies from case to case, and cannot be set without reference to conditions in the industry involved.

One proposal not adopted at this stage was that of a negotiated floor price system for cotton textiles and for jute and coir products, to be combined with duty-free entry under the scheme; failure by developing country exporters to maintain a minimum price level at the EEC boundary would have led to the suspension of duty-free treatment. This would presumably have been similar in operation to provisions by the Community relating to fruit and vegetables imported from some of the Mediterranean and North African countries with which it maintains trade agreements. Such a system ensures access for ldc products while making certain that they do not compete on price with domestic goods, and in effect transfers tariff revenue from EEC coffers to traders (either to importers or to exporters, depending on how contracts are operated). It is clear, however, that for these products the Community members, under pressure from domestic industries, were not prepared to countenance such a system.

The EEC's preliminary proposals for a generalised preference scheme were sent to OECD in time to meet the 1 March 1969 deadline laid down by the OECD *ad hoc* working group. But the OECD work marked time: principally because no GSP proposals were submitted by either the USA or Japan until 'illustrative lists' were published by the USA in late July. By November 1969, preliminary GSP offers by all the developed countries which aimed to take part were sent via the OECD to the UNCTAD Trade and Development Board. It became possible for each developing country to assess the potential advantages of the offers, and to try to amend them where necessary. It was clear, however, that the hope expressed in the UNCTAD II resolution that 'the arrangements should enter into effect in early 1970' was not to be fulfilled.

Although the main substance of an EEC scheme was now on the

table, there were still many detailed areas – potentially crucial to the value of the scheme – where the Community's point of view was not settled. Some of these – e.g. the rules of origin which would be applied, the exact list of beneficiaries, and the length of time for which GSP schemes would run – were questions which would be settled through negotiation in the UNCTAD Special Committee and the OECD; others – e.g. whether and how tariff quotas on 'sensitive' products would be divided among Community members, whether ceilings on imports from individual developing countries should be lower than 50 per cent of overall tariff quotas – were 'internal' Community decisions which nevertheless would affect the international context.

The performance of other Western countries did not encourage the Community authorities, and the member states to take a liberal stance. In particular, by the start of the fourth session of the Special Committee on Preferences in April 1970, the US attitude (under the Nixon administration, with a more overtly protectionist attitude than the Democrats) appeared to have hardened. Most unfortunately for the Community, the USA once again made its offer conditional on the elimination of special preferences on GSP products, the abolition of reverse preferences, and the adoption of the unified scheme by all developed countries. Naturally, this made the EEC's attitude to 'going it alone' much more guarded.

NOTES

1 p. 39.
2 For an assessment of the reasons for this boycott, see R. Mayne *The Institutions of the European Community* pp. 42-48
3 David Coombes (*op.cit.*, p.162) has noted 'the importance of negotiation and bargaining in the decision-making process and the Commission's dependence on the support of member states and their representatives for sustaining progress in the development of the Community'.
4 Although the possible impact of GSP on the Associates would probably have been rather small anyway. (See Chapter 7)
5 But this provision was eventually applied in a highly arbitrary manner
6 At UNCTAD II, the Associates themselves were prime movers in the inclusion of demands for special measures for least developed countries and for advantages 'equivalent' to those of Yaoundé preferences to be assured in the GSP. (See below, p.). They regarded reverse preferences as a matter for them to decide upon themselves, and not for international negotiation.
7 *Agence Europe*, 4 January 1968.
8 This has been done in excluding Hong Kong from the GSP on textiles.
9 It will be recalled that the USA was the only Western donor country ever to suggest that Agricultural products should be included in a system in principle.
10 *Agence Europe*, 1 February 1968.

11 Resolution 21 (II) UNCTAD II, *Proceedings*, Vol.I, p. 38.

12 Eduardo Martino, then Commissioner for External Affairs, Jean-Francois Deniau, then Commissioner for External Trade, and Henri Rochereau, then Commissioner for Development Aid.

13 TD/B/300/R.1, *Report of the Special Committee on Preferences on the first part of its fourth session*, para. 367.

7. INFLUENCES AND PRESSURES ON THE COMMUNITY

Community policy makers were clearly subject to a wide variety of pressures and influences over the design of the GSP scheme. External pressures from non-Community developed countries in OECD and from developing countries in UNCTAD had considerable weight, as has been seen. But within the Community itself three main sources of pressure can be identified: the commitment to existing common policies with political and temporal priority over the GSP; industrial and agricultural lobby pressures; and national policies, themselves influenced by national lobbies. This chapter examines some of these sources of pressure.

Pre-existing Community Policies

The two main common policy areas where Community priorities were challenged by the move to establish a GSP were Association and the Common Agricultural Policy (CAP) – the only two areas where, at the time, relevant common policies existed. The CAP, through the variable levy system, affects external trade in competing agricultural products directly; but its effects on trade are logically secondary to its aim of organising and encouraging domestic farm production. The Association policy was, and still is to some extent, aimed at creating and preserving a special connection between the Community and a particular group of developing countries. The GSP was likely to cause strong conflicts of interest on both scores.

Association and the GSP

A comprehensive preference scheme, covering all processed and semi-processed goods as well as 'manufactures' strictly defined, was likely to deprive the eighteen Yaoundé Associates of preferential trading advantages which many of them regarded as significant and which might have been expected to grow. Associates were concerned not only to maintain existing preferences, but also to create conditions under which any new export-oriented processing or manufacturing ventures they might sponsor would still be assured of better terms in the Community market than those of other ldcs.

The potential conflict between the preferential access given by the EEC to exports from its African Associates and the aim of creating a wider preference scheme for all developing countries was made even sharper by the timing of events. The first Yaoundé Convention associating newly-independent ex-colonies of France and Belgium with the Community, which had come into force on 1 June 1964, was due to expire and be renewed in 1969, when the OECD and UNCTAD discussions on the GSP were coming to a head. Clearly, the question of how a generalised system would affect the Associates' special preferences was likely to be a live issue in the 1968/69 Association talks.

In 1969, 80 per cent of AASM exports to the Community (summarised in Tables 7.1 and 7.2) were either agricultural or mineral products. Exports of minerals such as copper, diamonds, iron ore, aluminium, phosphates, petroleum, manganese, uranium, tin and wolfram were of pre-eminent importance to Zaïre, Mauritania, and the Central African Republic and of significant importance to Gabon, Congo Brazzaville and Rwanda. Apart from these minerals the principal AASM exports, in descending order of importance, were coffee, saw logs and veneer sheets, cocoa beans, cotton, groundnuts, groundnut and palm oils and oilcakes, cocoa butter and pineapples.

Most of the major minerals entered the Community market duty-free from all sources, as did saw logs, cotton, oilseeds and oilseed cakes. On these, therefore, the AASM received no preferences. The major agricultural products benefiting from preferential access ranged from palm and palm kernel oils (4 per cent preference) which were of importance principally to Zaïre and Dahomey, to canned pineapples and pineapple juice (32 per cent preference in 1969), of significance mainly to Ivory Coast. Most of those which could be counted as processed agricultural goods (principally groundnut oil, palm and palm kernel oils, cocoa butter and canned pineapples) were products in which the main competition for AASM producers came from other ldcs, and on which, therefore, Associates might be expected to press against the introduction of a GSP scheme by the Community. Although these processed products accounted for only some AASM exports to the Community, they formed significant proportions of the trade of Senegal and Niger, while Ivory Coast and Cameroun, two of the AASM countries with the closest links with France, could see essential interests as being eroded by the further extension of preferences. GSP terms were, in fact, withheld in the original EEC scheme on all these products.

The African Associates were in a better position than any other group of ldcs to make their views known to the Community authorities. Apart from maintaining diplomatic missions in Brussels they take part in joint institutions set up under the Association in which the 'Community side' and the 'Associates side' are represented on a basis of 'parity'.[1] At the top is the Association Council, composed of the members of the Council of the European Communities and members of the Commission of the European Communities and of a member of the

Table 7.1 YAOUNDE ASSOCIATES' TRADE PATTERN 1969

	Value of Exports ($ m)	Proportion to EEC (%)	Principal products (% of Total)
Burundi (1968	16	15	Coffee (56)
Cameroun	228	74	Cocoa (28) coffee (20) aluminium (10) timber (7) cocoa butter (8)
Central African Rep.	36	65	Diamonds (44) cotton (25) coffee (14)
Chad	31	84	Cotton (80)
Congo (Brazzaville)	44	59	Timber (50) diamonds (16) veneer sheets (11) sugar (7)
Dahomey	27	60	Palm kernel oil (22) cotton (11) palm oil (7) oil cakes (4) coffee (4)
Gabon	142	51	Petroleum (34) timber (3) manganese (19) uranium (5)
Ivory Coast	458	63	Coffee (25) cacao (22) saw logs (25), many minor products including cotton, pineapples.
Malagasy Republic	113	44	Coffee (28) spices (14) rice (8) sugar (5)
Mali	17	17	Live cattle (35) cotton (23) groundnuts (3)
Mauritania	76	47	Iron ore (90) fish (5)
Niger	24	68	Groundnuts (58) live animals (8) cotton (4) groundnut oil (4)
Rwanda	14	32	Coffee (42) tin (28) wolfram (14) tea (7)
Senegal	124	71	Groundnut oil (29) groundnuts (13) oil cakes (12) phosphates (9) fish (6)
Somalia	30	33	Live animals (50) bananas (23) hides (7) charcoal (3)
Togo	45	86	Cocoa beans (35) phosphates (28) coffee (15)
Upper Volta	20	17	Live animals (35) cotton (30) oilseeds (10)
Zaïre	644	54	Copper (67) diamonds (5) palm and kernel oils (5) coffee (4) other ores (3) rubber (2)
TOTAL	2089	55	

Source: EEC and UN statistics

Table 7.2

PREFERENTIAL TERMS FOR MAJOR YAOUNDE EXPORTS TO EEC, 1969

	% of preference
1. Coffee (8 countries, $ 124m. exports)	7
2. Sawlogs (4 countries, $ 155m.)	0
3. Cocoa beans (3 countries, $ 149m.)	4-5
4. Cotton (7 countries, $ 49m.)	0
5. Oilseeds & oilseed cakes (3 countries, $ 26m.)	0
6. Groundnut oil (2 countries, $ 36m.)	5
7. Palm and palmkernel oils (2 countries, $ 23m.)	4
8. Cocoa butter (1 country, $ 13m.)	12
9. Canned pineapples & juice (1 country, $ 8m.)	32
10. Fresh pineapples (1 country, $ 2m.)	9

Total above = $ 585m. (1)
Grand total of Yaoundé exports to EEC = $ 1,153m. (2)
(1) as % of (2) = 51%
Total above minus exports from Zaire = $ 567m. (3)
Grand total minus exports from Zaire = $ 877m. (4)
(3) as % of (4) = 65%

Source: EEC statistics

government of each associated state,[2] meeting at least once a year but in practice whenever necessary,[3] and with the powers to take binding decisions and to make 'such resolutions, recommendations or opinions as it may deem necessary to achieve the common objectives and to ensure the smooth functioning of the Association arrangements.'[4] It is also required periodically to review the results of the Association arrangements.[5] The Council is assisted by an Association Committee of officials, one from each EEC member, one from the Commission and one from each Associate, and maintains a small secretariat in Brussels. The institutional side of the Association is completed by a consultative Parliamentary Conference (which normally meets once a year) and a Court of Arbitration consisting of four independent judges, two nominated by each side, and a President appointed by the Association Council. Its function is to resolve disputes which the Association Council cannot settle. It has never acted so far.

Under Article 12 of the first Yaoundé Convention, the two sides agreed to keep each other informed on matters of commercial policy, and to consult at the request of either side on means of making the Association more effective. Three areas were particularly stressed: the suspension, alteration or abolition of customs duties, the granting of tariff quotas at reduced or zero duties, and the introduction, reduction or abolition of import quotas with respect to third countries, if these measures were likely to harm the interests of any EEC member or Yaoundé Associate. The extension of GSP fell in the centre of the area covered by this Article, and it was to be expected that the EEC would have to take account of the views of the Associates in framing the GSP. The coincidence in time of the 'peak' of GSP negotiations with those for the renewal of the Yaoundé Convention brought the issues involved even more sharply into focus. Not only were the Associates' attitudes to the GSP involved; the debate opened up the division within the Community itself between those member states, mainly the Netherlands and Germany, which wanted to make the ties of the Association more flexible in favour of a world approach to the problem of development, and those, led by France with its close ties with the majority of the associated states, which preferred to keep most of the Community's trade concessions for the AASM.

At UNCTAD II, the Yaoundé group had endorsed the Charter of Algiers. The Charter's discussion of generalised preferences included two specific provisions related directly to the interests of this group: firstly, that any GSP should be constructed in such a way that 'the least advanced among developing countries might benefit from it',[6] and secondly, that any GSP should ensure 'at least equivalent advantages' to developing countries which already benefited from preferences in developed countries (i.e. mainly the Commonwealth and Yaoundé states) to enable these special preferences to be suspended.[7]

What exactly 'equivalent advantages' means is not clear. The developing countries concerned may have been seeking some form of compensation (e.g. in a commitment to extra aid) for the loss of their special Commonwealth or Yaoundé privileges. At least, the ldcs proposed, the GSP should include duty-free access for all processed and semi-processed primary products exported by developing countries. But the developed countries maintained the stand – which the ldcs had in the end to accept – that the extension of GSP schemes by all developed countries be regarded as adequate compensation for the loss of special preferential privileges. However, their insistence that the GSP should principally apply only to 'manufactures' in BTN chapters 25-99 meant the omission of a large number of the processed goods in which many ldcs – including Associates as well as other less industrially advanced countries – might be interested, while the inability of the United States to introduce a GSP meant that Associates were unlikely to receive compensation for any potential loss of Community preferences, in terms of easier entry to the United States, the only other market of comparable size to the EEC Associates had, therefore, two connected and apparently valid reasons for wanting to hold on to and strengthen their special EEC preferences.[8]

The 1968/9 Association renegotiations formally began on 19 December 1968 in Brussels. The Associates' initial position was that the tariff preferences extended in their favour by the Community should be maintained, and even strengthened. This was supported by the Association Committee, which in a report originally adopted in October 1968 and sent to the EEC/AASM Parliamentary Conference meeting in January 1969 stated that:

> 'it would be desirable at least to maintain the present preferences in favour of Associates, preferences which have not in fact hindered the normal development of Community trade with other developing countries . . . If there was a generalisation of preferences for finished and semi-finished products from all developing countries, it would be desirable that preferential treatment be reserved for the Associated States.'[9]

The Parliamentary Conference itself stressed that regional preferences should not be reduced except in exchange for corresponding advantages.

Within the Community, France was the main supporter of this stand. It also had important private support from the then President of the Council of Ministers, Mr Gaston Thorn of Luxembourg; in May 1969, in a private intervention in the Association Parliamentary Conference, he made what was described as 'a vigorous plea against the tendency to dissolve the association in a world preference system'.[10] Mr Thorn maintained that there were two main trains of thought on the future of the Association within the Community. The first, 'supported by the minority',[11] would aim in the medium term to align the trading system of the Association with one which would apply to all developing countries; the second, 'defended by the majority of the member states',[12] would, 'envisage the permanent coexistence of the two preferential systems, the one for the benefit of all developing countries, and the other – more accentuated – for the benefit of the AASM. The association should not, therefore, stand in the way of the establishment of the generalised preference scheme under negotiation in the UNCTAD context, but this general system should not prevent the continuation of the association policy'.[13]

To the extent that none of the Associates' major processed agricultural exports were included in the scheme introduced in 1971, the pressure, supported by France, may be said to have succeeded. But one must also note that the provisions of the second Yaoundé Convention on AASM preferences were phrased in much less specific terms than those of the first, and left the way open for the extension to other ldcs of the tariff treatment given by the Community to the Associates, subject only to 'consultations within the Association Council'.[14] (Appendix 7.1 compares the terms of the two Conventions in this field – the second Convention much less rigid than the first.)

The CAP interest

Broadly speaking, pressure from Associates to limit the scope of the GSP was much less effective than the limits through member states' own perceptions of their needs for agricultural protection in the CAP. From the start, as has been noted, it was accepted that if processed products were included, the only part of the protective structure on which reductions would be given would be that which represented the protection of the processing industry: the part of the duty, or the levy, which was regarded as protecting domestic farm production would not be reduced.

Under the EEC's protective structure, processed agricultural goods can be divided into three groups; those on which only import duties under the Common External Tariff (CET) are levied, those on which import duties and CAP variable levies are charged, and those on whch CAP levies only are charged. Under the Yaoundé conventions, the Community has committed itself to giving Associates access on terms which are 'more favourable than the general treatment applied to like products originating in third countries'.[15] But this treatment varies widely from freedom from import duties and levies (on canned pineapples), through exemption from import duties, but not from CAP levies (on such items as beef and grapefruit segments), to no preferential terms whatsoever (on sugar and dairy products – perhaps the two most sensitive products of the Common Agricultural Policy.)[16] New concessions have been difficult even for Associates to negotiate: horticultural produce is a case in point. In this area, a prolonged dispute arose in 1972 between the EEC authorities and the African Associates over imports of vegetables – currently an insignificant amount in all, but a field in which some African countries (Kenya among the present Commonwealth Associates is the best example) see good prospects for exports to Europe, principally in the European winter. The Community took the attitude, initially, that no tariff-free access for such produce at all could be permitted; it was only in 1973, after prolonged negotiations reaching the level of a possible submission to the Association Court of Arbitration[17] that the Associates gained the right to export their produce duty-free to the Community during short, specified, 'off season' times of year.[18]

The Community applied four general rules – at least two of which were aimed, fairly evidently, at protecting EEC domestic output – to the treatment of processed agricultural goods under the GSP. First, no basic products or those which had undergone only simple processing, such as drying, smoking or decorticating, should be included, since the scheme was only intended to apply to manufactured or semi-manufactured products. Second, products subject only to CAP levies – i.e. principally grain and vegetable starches – must be excluded. The rationale, in this case, was the inability to identify the component of a CAP variable levy which represented 'industrial protection' – the Commission arguing that as a general principle, agricultural production had been protected under the CAP by the variable levy system, while CET customs duties (or their equivalent, the fixed component of a two-part levy) were intended for the protection of industry. Third, preferences were not to be offered on products which competed with food processing industries in the Community and in which developing countries could be shown to be strongly competitive. Lastly, no preferences were given on products on which Associates themselves did not benefit from preferential access to the Community market (i.e. mainly meat products, wheat and rye flour, olives and sugar; the last being the most important ldc product involved, and one which from the inception of the CAP had been ruled out of access to the EEC metropolitan countries).

Industrial Pressures

General Community-level action – UNICE

Apart from generally liberal attitudes taken by German importers, the balance of active pressure on the Community authorities and national governments from industrial interests was against the GSP. This is not surprising. Import liberalisation, however much it may increase general economic welfare, is seen as a threat to previously protected sectors of industry and may harm employment and investment prospects in specific sectors. The greatest pressure against liberalisation has not unnaturally come from those sectors of industry which are relatively uncompetitive or which are in any case going through changes in their production structure for other reasons; the textiles industry – or at least the part of it founded on production of the more traditional cotton fabrics and piece goods, in which developing countries have gained a decided cost advantage – has been a major case.

The possibility of a GSP being introduced caused a particularly strong reaction from industries for two main reasons. First, industrial interests not involved in overseas production were very much against the conclusion of a deal involving one-way concessions to exports from developing countries, and particularly the principle of 'self election' to the list of beneficiary ldcs. This was seen as opening Community markets to some of EEC industries' strongest competitors (including many British, American and Japanese-owned firms in developing countries) without the possibility of better treatment in ldc markets for Community-based exporters. This argument was backed up by the plea that imports from low-wage economies would disrupt EEC markets, harming employment and growth in 'sensitive' regions and sectors.

At the Community level, the general industrial viewpoint on the GSP was put forward by UNICE *(L'Union des Industries de la Communauté Européenne),* a joint body formed by the industrial federations of the Six member states to 'represent them at the Community level and within which the general problems raised by the application of the Treaties of Rome could be discussed'.[19]

As a federation of federations composed of bodies with widely differing interests UNICE cannot easily take a detailed stance on particular issues. Individual industries maintain their own pressure groups at Community level as well as nationally. 'At Community level, pressure groups belong to two broad categories: one cutting right across internal boundaries, the other roughly synonymous with national interests of member countries. Both these categories have political as well as socio-economic connotations and in both conservative voices alternate with progressive . . . Last but not least are the hundred and more "European" trade associations which, ever since the Community's inception, began to open offices on or off the rue de la Loi'.[20] UNICE's memoranda are thus concerned more with the way in which broad issues of policy rebound on industry, than with detail.

The association's attitude to the GSP was first set out in a memorandum dated January 1968, which stressed the need for safeguards against 'market disruption', for 'objective criteria' in choosing the beneficiaries of the GSP, and for participation in the GSP by as many developed countries as possible, in order to share the 'burden' in an equitable way. The main points of UNICE's case were:

1. In general terms, GATT rules 'which admit to preferential treatment only in exceptional and well defined situations'[21] were seen to be respected; generalised preferences should therefore be clearly seen as a definite exception to GATT rules governed by a waiver from GATT, and should be temporary and degressive with an initial period of five years. They should not call into question the free trade areas established between the EEC and the Yaoundé Associates.

2. While GSP access might have considerable psychological value for the ldc beneficiaries, UNICE was not convinced that preferences would, on their own, have any certain positive effects on the growth of ldcs' exports (a point made by the Commission in its first memorandum on the GSP, in 1966). Nevertheless, it was, in their view, important not to extend preferential access unconditionally to ldcs, in order to avoid the 'grave economic disruption' to which developed countries would be exposed and which would rebound on the developing countries by harming the prosperity of the developed world and hence diminishing the volume of aid that rich countries could give.

3. Thus, safeguard clauses introduced by developed countries in the GSP context should aim to protect not only their own production *but also their imports from other industrialised countries.* Such safeguards should go beyond simple anti-dumping measures to restrict *ex ante* the volume of duty-free imports from developing countries. Essentially, the GSP should consist internationally of a system of tariff quotas divided among the donor countries, and preferential treatment should be withdrawn from imports from ldcs which rose above a given proportion of the tariff quota, in order to ensure that less competitive developing countries had a 'fair' share.

4. As a further safeguard, beneficiary.countries and products should be carefully selected according to 'objective criteria'.[22] Developing

countries should be divided into distinct categories treated more or less restrictively depending on the competitiveness of their industries; and 'sensitive' products should also be excluded from the scheme.

5. The GSP must be organised on a world-wide basis, including the developing countries as preference-givers themselves; preferences among ldcs, it was argued, would increase the effectiveness of measures aimed at raising the level of exports from these countries.

It is clear from the first UNICE memorandum that the official reaction of industries in the Community, as a group, was, if not overtly hostile to the idea of a GSP, very lukewarm. As the proposals became more concrete the UNICE attitude became more openly critical. Its second memorandum,[22] issued in reply to the Commission's proposal in February 1969 to submit its GSP in outline to the OECD, spoke of 'grave anxieties' being aroused in many industries and re-stressed four main points: that tariff preferences should only be extended to non-competitive countries and products; that the self-election principle should be rejected in favour of leaving the Community free to exclude given countries, products or *products from specific countries* from the system; that a safeguard clause be established allowing to EEC even to limit preferential access to levels even lower than predetermined tariff quotas, if 'market disruption' were proved; and that the level of tariff cut to be applied should vary from product to product, rather than allowing general tariff-free access even within tariff quotas.

By 1971, when it became clear that the Community was likely to introduce its scheme before the other main donors, UNICE's line had become even harder. The association's third statement on GSP in February 1971[24] found it 'totally unacceptable' that the Community should put into effect the benefits the GSP offered to ldcs, without being certain that all other industrial countries were also doing so at the same time. It deplored the fact that all members of the Group of 77 were without distinction or exception to benefit from the scheme. It thought that the GSP should not be applied to state-trading countries such as Rumania, Bulgaria and Cuba with 'incompatible' export pricing policies, and that the conditions to be applied to Hong Kong and Macao – given, regrettably, that these territories were to be included at all – should be stricter than to any other ldcs. Ceilings applied to them should be lower, most sensitive products excluded and stronger rules of origin applied if these territories were to be included.

Although it is difficult to assess the impact of any one pressure group on the Community's policy, UNICE's lobbying – at least insofar as its memoranda are concerned – appears to have been rather ineffectual. There are two reasons. It is unlikely that a campaign as broadly based and unconnected to specific issues concerning well-defined 'sensitive' sectors of industry would be successful, given the Community's commitment – by the time of the first memorandum – to going ahead with a non-selective preference scheme along with its OECD partners, under pressure from the developing countries. Again, the direction of UNICE pressure was not very likely to get its views substantially endorsed. UNICE's main direction of contact with the Community institutions is with the EEC Commission; formal and informal meetings take place at various levels – between Commissioners and the UNICE Council of Presidents (the formal policy-making body for UNICE composed of the presidents of the national federations involved in UNICE): between the permanent delegates to UNICE and Commission staff 'to seek information either on questions that might interest industry, or on the evolution of the problems on which UNICE has already taken up a position':[25] between the members of expert committees set up by UNICE and the relevant departments of the Commission. 'In some cases . . . representatives of the Commission participate in the work of UNICE, in order to explain to the experts of the industrial Federations the content of the proposals of the Commission on which UNICE envisages giving an opinion'.[26] But its contacts with the Council are much less regular and influential than the pressures put on national governments by industries based in the member states. As has been seen, the Commission (from 1966 onwards) was the main proponent of a relatively liberal policy on GSP among the Community institutions, and the department of the Commission most closely concerned (DG I) one of the most liberal elements in the Commission structure. UNICE pressures across the spectrum of industry, without any particular focus, would have been unlikely to reach many very sympathetic ears within the Commission. But the UNICE campaign did serve to reinforce national efforts by industry lobbies.

A Successful Case : the Textile Industry

At the Community level, the textile industry as a whole is represented by COMITEXTIL, the Co-ordinating Committee for the Textile Industries in the European Economic Community. This body brings together the national federations of textile firms of the Community as well as the Community-wide associations of the cotton, wool, jute, hard and coconut fibre, yarn spinning, throwing and texturing, knitwear, carpets and furnishings, lace, embroidery, curtains, ribbons and elastic, and printing industries. Each association sent, before EEC enlargement, six[27] delegates to general meetings of COMITEXTIL – 120[2] in all, in the original Community. The clothing industry – apart from knitwear interests – does not participate in COMITEXTIL but has its own federation. The association is governed by a management council of 40 which controls a General Secretariat responsible, in turn, for a large number of working groups in which national industry representatives take part, falling under five main headings – Industrial Matters, Foreign Trade, Statistics and Economic Research, Scientific and Technological Research, and Information, Press and External Relations.

Large sections of the textile industry in most developed countries have, over the past decade, found themselves highly sensitive, and increasingly so, to competition from outside sources and particularly from developing countries. Textile interests in Britain, the Community and the USA have for many years been lobbying strongly, and with a fair measure of success to maintain or increase protection against these imports. Initially the main sector facing serious pressure from imports was the cotton weaving industry.

In common with textile representatives in other developed areas, COMITEXTIL was, and is, particularly concerned with the growth of imports of manufactured textiles and clothing from the Far East; particularly from Hong Kong, Taiwan and Macao. The Community's balance of trade in clothing had consistently been in surplus of over $200m. from 1959 until 1968, when it began to fall, reaching a deficit of $19m. by 1971 (Table 7.4). A number of developing countries had been increasing their share of the Community's imports of clothing; notably Hong Kong (the EEC's largest external supplier, with 25 per cent of extra Community imports in 1971), and Taiwan, while imports under bilateral agreements from Yugoslavia and Rumania accounted for a further 18.5 per cent of imports in 1971 (Table 7.5). COMITEXTIL's annual survey of the EEC textile industry for 1971 noted that 'the industrialised countries' share (of clothing imports into the EEC), which had been 50 per cent in 1968, fell to 37.8 per cent in 1970 and 30 per cent in 1971, whereas that of class 2 (developing) countries, in the same period, rose from 30.3 per cent to 36.7 per cent and that of class 3 (state-trading) countries from 19.1 per cent to 32.5 per cent. *It follows that more than two-thirds of our clothing imports come from countries with abnormally low prices'.*[28] Another COMITEXTIL publication noted that on the world scale 'the most important phenomenon is unquestionably the considerable growth (in exports) of Asiatic countries. India showed a 31 per cent increase and confirmed its rank as sixth world exporter. Taiwan showed a quite marked increase . . . thanks to her exports' progress by 43 per cent (79 per cent for clothing articles) . . . It can be estimated that the five so-called developing countries listed here (Hong Kong, South Korea, Taiwan, India and Pakistan) must have represented in 1971 only for the five of them, more than 80 per cent of the total exports from developing countries, compared to 72 per cent in

Table 7.3 Intra-EEC trade in textiles, 1958, 1969 and 1971

	Value			Annual	Growth
	1958	1969 US$ million	1971	1958/69	1969/71
1 Total textiles					
Intra-EEC trade	725	4,262	5,533	20.4	14.0
Exports to third countries	1,566	2,919	3,525	6.0	10.0
Imports from third countries	1,731	2,747	2,999	4.3	4.5
Extra-trade balance	-165	+172	+526		
2 Raw materials					
Intra-EEC trade	163	506	515	10.6	0.8
Exports to third countries	203	349	330	4.6	-2.8
Imports from third countries	1,383	1,462	1,233	0.4	-8.9
Extra-trade balance	-1,180	-1,113	-903		
3 Manufactures					
Intra-EEC trade	452	2,482	3,174	17.3	13.2
Exports to third countries	1,109	1,936	2,472	5.2	13.0
Imports from third countries	292	821	1,025	9.8	11.7
Extra-trade balance	+807	+1,115	+1,447		
4 Clothing					
Intra-EEC trade	110	1,274	1,844	24.9	20.3
Exports to third countries	253	634	723	8.7	6.8
Imports from third countries	156	464	742	10.4	26.5
Extra-trade balance	+197	+170	-19		

Source: 'The textile industry of the European Community: Balance Sheet and annual survey' COMITEXTIL *Documents* 73/1, February 1973.

Table 7.4 EEC textile imports from developing countries, 1969 - 1971

	Value 1969	Value 1971	Share of extra-EEC imports	Share of total EEC trade
	US$ million		% in 1971	
1 Total textiles	974	1,036	34.5	12.1
2 Raw materials of which:	623	464	37.6	26.5
Turkey	...	108	8.8	6.2
Brazil	...	43	3.5	2.5
Pakistan	...	42	3.4	2.4
China	...	38	3.1	2.1
3 Manufactures of which:	193	300	29.3	7.1
Greece	...	38	3.7	0.9
India	...	31	3.0	0.7
Pakistan	...	28	2.7	0.7
4 Clothing of which:	158	272	36.7	10.5
Hong Kong	114	183	24.7	7.1
Taiwan	17	22	3.0	0.9
Macao	16	21	2.8	0.8
S. Korea	5	13	1.8	0.5
Yugoslavia [1]	58	104	14.0	4.0
Romania [1]	...	33	4.5	1.3

Note: 1 Not included in clothing total.

Source: As Table 7.3.

1970. *It results from this that this evolution takes place to a large extent at the expense of real developing countries'.*[29] Thus, COMITEXTIL's continuing argument for protection rested on two bases; that the most competitive sources of supply had 'abnormally low' prices (although no specific evidence of dumping, or any other 'abnormality' of the type, appeared in the studies mentioned) and that restrictions on access from these countries could benefit 'real' ldcs whose textile industries were not so well developed or competitive.

If the first part of this argument rests on an arbitrary judgment of what is, or is not, 'abnormal' pricing, the second contains two straightforward *non sequiturs*, in the propositions that restriction on exports from countries whose export industries compete effectively with importers' domestic production will necessarily help less competitive countries to compete with this home output, and that the 'real' developing countries are necessarily the less competitive. Restriction on highly competitive exporters is only likely to be useful to others where an overall 'global' quantity limit, or a tariff quota, is enforced and filled completely by imports from one or two particularly large, competitive exporters. Here, restrictions on the dominant supplier countries may indeed give room for similar, but still competitive, exporters to enter the market. The Community GSP's buffer levels are a case in point. But there is little evidence that, in general, holding back competitive imports helps to promote new trade.

The textile producers' real aim was, clearly, to maintain the considerable advantages which the EEC customs union had given them through the protective tariff and free internal movement of goods. As Table 7.4 shows, during the period from EEC establishment up to 1971, intra-Community trade in textiles had increased over sevenfold, from $725m. to $5.5 billion. By 1969 – the year when the major decisions about the GSP were taken – it had already grown almost six times. Clothing and manufactured textiles' trade had contributed most to this growth: the 'threatened' clothing sector with an increase, in value terms, of intra-trade from $110m. to $1,844m. – nearly seventeenfold – in the period to 1971 (twelvefold to 1969), and textile manufactures with a sevenfold increase in the thirteen-year period. During the same period, exports of manufactured textiles to third countries – principally (65 per cent in 1971) other industrial nations – doubled, while exports of clothing nearly tripled.

Statistics expressed in terms of value only, however, are misleading, as they do not separate price and volume; and price competition, for the European textile industries most affected, was the main problem. Moreover, the prosperity or vulnerability of the industry varied enormously between member states, and between, and within, sectors of the industry. Broadly, the sectors which have done best in recent years have been those manufacturing luxury, or more complex, products such as carpets, fancy woollen goods and furnishing fabrics; while the 'classic' woven fabrics and clothing, as well as jute products, have found their profitability steadily eroded by foreign competition. Again, the broad situation of the industry varied greatly from country to country, with the German and Dutch industries generally more competitive and modern than those of France and Italy; and within each country pockets of prosperity and depression could also be identified. The need was to help the industry at large to restructure itself towards greater competivity.

At around the same time as the GSP was under discussion, the Industrial Affairs Directorate of the Commission had commissioned a major study[30] on the state of the EEC textile industry from Professor Jacques de Bandt, then assistant director of the Centre d'Etudes des Techniques Economiques Modernes (Ecole Pratique des Hautes Etudes – Paris).[31] The study, which covered the whole industry except the clothing sector, was not well received by the industry's representatives; perhaps (in part at least) because of its stated objective, which was to 'evaluate the worth of the great mass of resources engaged in the textile industry, while giving it its rightful place in the international division of labour'. De Bandt's study examined how far EEC textiles could face up to foreign competition – principally that of the developing countries; his main conclusion was that the industry as a whole could survive without protection if considerable restructuring were undertaken. His view was that some branches of the industry (e.g. hard fibres, jute) could not be maintained in the long term without protection: and that the maintenance of any activity in these sectors required a major conversion to other materials (e.g. polyolefins in the case of jute). The ageing report noted excess capacity, ageing capital equipment, and excessive stocks in parts of the industry, but, at the same time, productivity per worker growing faster than total production, except in the fields of chemical fibres and haberdashery. De Bandt estimated that overall, with no trade liberalisation and no further term changes in the conditions of the industry through growing external competition, total output in 1975 would be only some 30 per cent above the level of 1966, with a reduction in employment of some 19 to 20 per cent or some 310-330,000 employees. It was impossible to put a figure on the consequences of trade liberalisation except on totally arbitrary and extreme hypotheses.

De Bandt proposed, in broad terms, the elimination of excess capital equipment and the phasing out of unprofitable firms, in order to 'refurbish' the textile industry's capital stock; and, at the same time, the promotion of new investment in the industry and its reorganisation into a more integrated form. But, because it was not part of the brief, he could not examine the structure of the clothing sector in the same detail as other parts of the textile industry. Clothing accounted for about two-thirds of the output of the textile industry; 'the conditions under which the clothing sector operates are, in some respects, critical for the textile industry – to the extent that the clothing trade is either in control of or in permanent contact with final outlets.'[32] To de Bandt, the institutional separation of the two sectors was a grave handicap; the future of the two were necessarily linked, and the type of restructuring which he saw as necessary for the textile sector (opening of the Community market, vertical and horizontal integration) would have also to extend through to the clothing industry.

This report, with its overt aim of creating an industry which could compete at world level substantially without protection, was regarded by the industry as a charter for the Community authorities to dismantle textile production in the EEC in favour of low-cost, 'unfair' competition from abroad; and the Commission's proposals to include textiles in the 'no exceptions' GSP on manufactures (on whatever limited scale) were seen by the industry as merely a part of this process. COMITEXTIL commented on Commission proposals, set out in 1971, on the future of the textile industry in the following terms:-

> 'You know that none of our efforts to explain the data, no attempt to present the facts objectively, no warning against mistaken generalities, nothing has been able to overcome, up till now, the "anti-textile" prejudices of certain economic, political, or press circles . . .
>
> It is equally clear that there remain in the field or on orders powerful forces which will find in the Commission's proposals material to promote their free view of the "transfer" or "amputation" of the European textile industry.
>
> MOreover, the industry's wishes are not all taken into account in defining the policy, and many textile firms will feel that their own value and technical excellence has been singularly underestimated – even ignored . . .

The Commission's proposals had followed closely de Bandt's line on the need for industry to adapt to changing circumstances; they stated:

> '. . . the evolution of the textile sector towards increased and adequate competitiveness requires, at company level, the continuation and even the acceleration, of the restructuring movement already begun. This restructuring will proceed by concentration, conversion and obsolescence and will prove all the more necessary in that the application of new technologies (in the field of fibres, processing

> materials, products, and management), the utilization of which is indispensable, will require structural adaptation . . .'
> In the course of the forthcoming years the Community will be characterised by a gradual opening to imports and more especially those from the developing countries. The strengthening of healthy competition, both inside and outside the Community, will constitute the principal incentive to restructuring.[33]

The textile lobbies' efforts to influence the EEC Commission against the inclusion of textiles in the GSP were strongly supported at national level; for example, in West Germany, where a group of Bundestag members representing textile- and jute-manufacturing constituencies mounted an attack on the GSP through questions in the Bundestag to the Minister of Finance and through a lobby of the German members of the European Parliament. Questions focussed on the fear that the industry would be opened up to 'the largest, most competitive and cheapest suppliers of the world market in textiles – who need no preferences'[34] and urged the government to bring in a system of differential reductions in tariffs instead of one of duty-free tariff quotas. The Commission and the Council of Ministers were accused of a frivolous attitude to the possibility of dumping, tariff evasion and corruption, and of taking steps which would lead to the bankruptcy certainly of some sectors of the industry in particular regions. The German government was able to withstand most of the charges without great difficulty; but made two major points in defence of its attitude. First, the need for an annual revision of the scheme, as a safeguard, was stressed. Second, and more substantially, the government undertook 'to bring it about that the key *(the butoir)* is lowered from 50 per cent to a lesser amount'[35] on sensitive textile products imported from countries which might 'disrupt the German market by dumping'[36] textiles. At this stage, buffer levels of 50 per cent of overall tariff quotas had been proposed by the Commission for all manufactures included in the GSP. In the end, *butoirs* not only on textiles but also on most other sensitive products were fixed at 30 per cent or below tariff quota levels. There is no doubt that the German government's attitude had an important bearing on the decision; and it is probable that once a low general level of *butoir* had become accepted in the 'super- sensitive' area of textiles a bandwagon of claims for similar sensitive treatment for other products would get under way. The German attitude, too, makes plain once again the real protective reason for the low level of *butoir*, as against the publicly stated rationale of safeguarding the interests of weaker developing countries.

The German attitude to the operation of tariff quotas on textiles contrasts strangely, at first sight, with the liberal image generally presented by German trade policy. The underlying reason was political. In the second half of 1970, a year after it had taken office, the Brandt government was at its weakest in Parliament. Although important initiatives taken by the new government in the fields of relations with Eastern Europe and with East Germany in particular were coming to fruition; its popularity nationally was not assured; and domestic economic policy was in difficulties. The parliamentary majority of the governing coalition was cut from twelve to six by the defection of three Free Democrat members of the Opposition; and despite favourable results in local elections in Hess and Bavaria the Social/Free Democrat coalition's position was still not strong. In the circumstances the government was in no position to antagonise any sector of its support or to take action which could be construed as weakening the economy. Textile imports were one issue where pressure could be easily applied both from a regional angle and on 'Community burden-sharing' grounds, given that West Germany was already the most overtly liberal of the Six in its attitude to imports and had the highest level of import penetration.[37]

It may be that the abandonment of relative liberalism on preferences was seen as part of a domestic political horse-trade for a degree of freedom to carry on foreign policy aims *(Ostpolitik)* which the Brandt government saw as more important. It is, moreover, the kind of move that, concealed in the *mélange* of an EEC Council position on preferences, could go by without seriously harming the government's generally liberal image. Whatever the reasons for the move, there is no doubt that West Germany's attitude to the GSP – at least as far as textiles were concerned – was manifestly not as liberal when details were hammered out as when general principles were being determined.

Appendix 7.1 A Comparison of Article 2 of the First and Second Yaoundé Conventions.

1. Yaoundé I Article 2

'1. Goods originating in Associated States, shall, when imported into Member States, benefit from the progressive abolition of customs duties and charges having an effect equivalent to such duties, resulting between Member States under the provisions of Articles 12, 13, 14, 15, and 17 of the Treaty and the decisions which have been or may be adopted to accelerate the rate of achieving the aims of the Treaty.

2. Nevertheless, upon the entry into force of the Convention, Member States shall abolish the customs duties and charges having an effect equivalent to such duties which they apply to the goods originating in Associated States which are listed in the Annex to this Convention. (i.e. fresh pineapples, desiccated coconut, coffee, tea, pepper, vanilla, cloves, nutmeg, cocoa beans).

At the same time Member States shall apply the common customs tariff duties of the Community to imports of these goods from third countries'.

2. Yaoundé II Article 2

'1. Products originating in the Associated States shall, on importation into the Community, be admitted free of customs duties and charges having equivalent effect, but the treatment applied to these products may not be more favourable than that applied by the Member States among themselves'.[1]

NOTES

1. 'Parity' implies the need for the Associates to take a common standpoint on any issue on which the EEC has one official attitude; Art. 45 of the second Yaoundé Convention thates that

   > The Association Council shall act by mutual agreement between the Community on the one hand and the Associated States on the other. The Community on the other hand and the Associated States on the other shall each by means of an internal protocol determine their procedure for arriving at their respective positions.

2. *Yaoundé II* Article 42.
3. *Ibid.*, Article 44.
4. *Ibid.*, Article 46.
5. *Ibid.*, Article 46.
6. Charter of Algiers, Programme of Action, Section B, para (f), UNCTAD II, Proceedings, Vol,I, p. 434, United Nations, 1968. Among specific proposals made by the ldc's in this area were for flexible time limits for the operation of the GSP, assurances that escape clauses or tariff quotas would not be applied to 'the less competitive products from less advanced countries', and special technical assistance and financial aid for the establishment of export-oriented industries in the least developed countries.
7. Charter of Algiers, Section B, para (g).
8. An article by Alassane D. Ouattara, 'Trade Effects of the Association of African Countries with the European Economic Community' (IMF *Staff Papers,* July 1973) suggests that AASM countries had already lost out, as far as their preferential access to France was concerned.
9. EEC/AASM Parliamentary Conference *Report* January 1969.
10. *Agence Europe,* 23 May 1969.
11. *Ibid*
12. *Ibid*
13. *Ibid*
14. Yaoundé Convention II, Article 15
15. Yaoundé Convention, 1969, Protocol 1.
16. See Frank Ellis, John Marsh and Christopher Ritson, *Farmers and Foreigners,* ODI, 1973.
17. See p. 69.
18. See Ellis *et al., op cit.,* p. 13. The only periods during which duty-free access is allowed for Associates are the months of May, October and November.
19. UNICE Explanatory Memorandum (undated). In the EEC before enlargement UNICE was composed of delegates from the Bundesverband der Deutschen Industrie and Bundesvereinigung der Deutschen Arbeitgeberverbande; the Federation des Industries Belges (now renamed Federation des Entreprises Belges, reflecting its broader scope); the Conseil National du Patronat Français; the Confederazione Generale dell' Industria Italiana; the Federation des Industriels Luxembourgeois; the Verbond van Nederlandse Ondermeningen and the Nederlands Christelijk Werkgeversverbond. The British CBI has been a member of UNICE since the enlargement of the Community. UNICE's aims are described as 'to maintain and foster the spirit and links of solidarity among its members, to encourage the elaboration of an industrial policy in a European spirit; and to be the official spokesman of the industries of the Six countries *vis-a-vis* the Common Market institutions for all problems of general interest or related

to matters of principle concerning the common policy of the central federations of industry'.

20. Götz Schoffer and Georges Micholet-Coté, 'The Indian Trade of the European Community: Attitudes, Policies and Trends', Royal Institute of International Affairs conference paper, mimeo, September 1972, p. 5.
21. UNICE Memorandum 19A.4, 24 January 1968: "Octroi eventuel de préférences tarifaires pour les produits manufacturés et semi-manufacturés des pays en voie de developpement". (Translated by the author.)
22. Proposals were made along these lines by the Commission in outlining the scheme for 1974, but were never adopted.
23. UNICE Memorandum 19 A.4: 'Octroi de Préférences . . .', 27 February 1969.
24. UNICE Memorandum 10.A.4/19 A.4: 'Préférence Tarifaires', 1 February 1971.
25. 'The Union of Industries of the European Community' mimeo, August 1971, p. 10.
26. *Ibid*
27. Now nine.
27a. Now 180
28. 'The Textile Industry of the European Community, Balance sheet and annual survey', COMITEXTIL Documents 73/1, February 1973 (Author's italics).
29. 'EEC Textile Industry and World Economy' COMITEXTIL Documents 72/9, 1972.
30. 'L'Industrie Textile de la CEE, Analyse et Perspectives' (1975), Rapport presenté a la Commission des Communautés Europeénes par le Professeur J. de Bandt, Janvier 1969 (Mimeo) p. 200.
31. Now Director of the Institut de Recherches en Economie de la Production, (IREP), Nanterre, Paris.
32. *Ibid.*, p. 215.
33. 'The textile industry of tomorrow: trends for a textile policy according to the EEC Commission's report', COMITEXTIL Bulletin No. 7/8, 1971.
34. Deutsche Bundestag, Official Report, Thursday 12 November 1970. Questions by Representatives Van Delden, Seiters, Ott and Fuchs, to the Minister of Finance.
35. *Ibid.*, p. 4463: Reply by Mr Rosenthal, Parliamentary Secretary to the Ministry of Finance, to question by Representative Seiters.
36. *Ibid.*, p. 4463, Question by Mr Seiters.
37. Cf. Britain's attitude to EEC textile imports in 1973-4: namely, that unrestricted internal movement of textiles was important to ensure that the burden of imports was evenly spread within the Community.

8. PROBLEMS WITH THE GSP

A tariff-cutting scheme like the GSP is, in theory at least, intended to provide financial benefits to the 'beneficiary' developing countries, both by increasing the profitability of exports of manufactures and processed goods and by creating an incentive to expand exports to the 'donor' countries. Chapter 3 has noted that there may be trade-creating or trade-diverting effects, depending on whether preferential imports compete with domestic manufactures or replace imports from other sources. The benefits to developing countries to which the tariff cuts apply may be the same in either case: their aim is to create new exports, or expand existing ones, no matter how. But trade creation may operate to the short-term cost of weak, uncompetitive domestic industries which previously sheltered behind tariff barriers: hence, pressure to exclude particular goods from the GSP, to limit access by tariff quotas, or to introduce new safeguards against 'market disruption'.

Again, tariff cuts for all developing countries (preferential or not) are, rather obviously, likely to benefit the more advanced 'industrialising' countries first, or more than the less developed. If this is the case, may (or can) action to help the poorer, less competitive ldcs be taken through the provisions of the GSP: or are quite different types of policies (e.g. increased aid, long-term trade contracts, reductions in NTBs) more suitable?

It has also been noted in Chapter 3 that for many products the enlargement of the EEC and its attendant free trade area with EFTA countries means that *preferential* access may be meaningless because ldcs main competitors will be trading on unrestricted free-trade terms. When can ldcs do to ensure that, in these circumstances, their processed and manufactured goods have a reasonable chance of competing in the Community market?

Initial Criticisms of the EEC Scheme

The GSP scheme originally introduced by the Six was heavily criticised for the limitations it placed on the expansion of ldc exports. The main criticisms related to the scheme's limited product coverage, in particular on processed agricultural goods, and the small tariff reductions on those processed goods which were included; the effects of overall tariff quota ceilings and, even more, *butoirs* (buffer levels) in restricting the potential growth of exports; the arbitrary division of tariff quotas among the EEC member states and the differing methods used by individual members to administer them; and the restrictive rules of origin.

The UNCTAD Secretariat brought out many of the initial problems of the EEC scheme in a survey issued in January 1973 as part of the general review of GSP schemes undertaken for the fifth meeting of the Special Committee on Preferences.[1] Factual analysis was hampered by the absence of hard statistics for the period during which the scheme had been in force. In principle, however, it appeared likely that only some 23 per cent of dutiable imports from ldcs into the Six could benefit from GSP access (Table 8.1). A relatively high proportion of BTN 25-99 products (64 per cent) could look forward to duty-free treatment, provided they could pass the rules of origin and did not come up against tariff quotas or *butoirs:* but only 1.8 per cent, at best, of dutiable imports in BTN 1-24 were estimated to be eligible for the scheme's relatively small preferential margins.

TABLE 8.1

1970 IMPORTS OF PRODUCTS COVERED BY EEC's 1972 SCHEME
$m

	Products in category:		
	BTN 1-24	BTN 25-99	BTN 1-99
Total imports from beneficiaries	3,090	9,250	12,340
Dutiable imports from beneficiaries	2,444	1,293	3,737
Dutiable as % of total imports	79	14	30
Imports covered by GSP:			
maximum	44	827	871
minimum	5	788	793
% of dutiable imports from beneficiaries covered by GSP:			
maximum	1.8	64	23
minimum	0.2	61	21

Source: UNCTAD document TD/B/C.5/3., Table 1.

The UNCTAD study also showed that, in aggregate, 'sensitive' and 'semi-sensitive' products were likely to form the greater part (some 67 per cent) of manufactures admitted to GSP treatment. For these products, moreover, global tariff quota and duty-free ceiling levels for 1972 were in aggregate some 16 per cent below the actual level of imports in 1970; so that on a normal growth rate of imports of manufacturers from ldcs, the actual discrepancy for 1972 would be even greater.

TABLE 8.2

EEC 1970 IMPORTS FROM BENEFICIARIES OF 'SENSITIVE', 'SEMI-SENSITIVE' AND 'NON-SENSITIVE' PRODUCTS IN THE 1972 GSP. ($ million)

Product groups	Imports covered by scheme				
	Sensitive		Semi-sensitive		Non-sensitive
	Value	Tariff Quota	Value	Duty-free ceiling	Value
LTA cotton textiles and substitutes	39.2	14.0	0.7	3.5	5.3
Other textiles and foot wear	149.2	128.6	3.1	3.5	14.4
ECSC iron and steel	32.3	28.4	3.3	3.3	0
All other manufactures and semi-manufactures	249.1	183.2	61.2	89.9	236.2
TOTAL	469.9	354.3	68.3	100.2	259.9

Source: TD/B/C. 5/3, Table 3.

The main impact of tariff quota barriers is likely to be on the expectations of parties involved in trade (purchasers, producers in the ldcs). The EEC Commission had argued, in designing a scheme based on *ex ante* tariff quotas, that the system had the great advantage of certainty: everyone involved knew on which products duty-free imports were likely to be strictly limited, and which ones were likely to be effectively freely importable – as against a 'safeguard clause' system where an importing government could apply the brakes to preferential imports in an arbirtary manner. But there is little doubt that the reverse was the case. True, traders in products which were openly designated as 'non-sensitive' could be fairly well assured that without substantial and successful pressure from threatened domestic producers, all would be well. But for sensitive products the situation was far from clear. All that could be expected at the start of any given year, by any producer or trader, was that at some point tariffs were likely to be reimposed on imports of the product in question from the countries concerned. When, and at what level of trade, tariffs would be reimposed depended on four factors; the overall size of the Community tariff quota for any sensitive product, the level of the *butoir*, the relative proportions of actual trade with each member state compared with the way in which tariff quotas were divided among the Six, and the way in which each member state administered its tariff quota system.

In practice, it appears that in 1972, *butoirs* were a much more effective limitation on duty-free imports of sensitive products than global tariff quotas; while the overall ceilings were more frequently effective on 'semi-sensitive' products (Table 8.3). Of the 16 items which hit the tariff quota ceilings in 1972[2] only three (yarn of discontinuous synthetic fibre, knitted garments, and trailers) were counted as sensitive. But the majority of sensitive products were affected by the *butoirs,* from mid-February 1972 onwards. Hong Kong and Yugoslavia were the two countries whose exports most frequently hit *butoir* levels (for 24 items from Yugoslavia, 22 from Hong Kong), and the number of cases where *butoirs* on the same products were reached by both countries, or where other countries than these two were also subject to *butoir* limits, was small. It is likely, therefore, that the *butoir* system did operate to the advantage of minor suppliers, as was intended (i.e. assuming that minor suppliers of the affected products existed); and unlikely that the operation of *butoirs* did in practice often prevent smaller suppliers from gaining entry under tariff quotas, as had been feared, as a result of two or three major suppliers pre-empting the whole tariff quota on any one item. The possibility, at least, of trade diversion from major to minor ldc suppliers existed under the scheme.

But the operation of the tariff quota system by the member states brought its own problems. Allocation on a 'first come, first served' basis of import licences (the greyhound method) as used in Benelux and increasingly in West Germany was in principle the more liberal. But it is also caused the greatest uncertainties. Neither exporters nor importers could be certain (unless they were monopolists) that a given consignment would arrive at the EEC port of entry before other imports had filled the tariff quota allocation; this uncertainty is underlined when one remembers that 1972's tariff quota on Indian cotton fabrics was exhausted by mid-February of that year. On the other hand, the system used by France and, initially, Germany of prior allocation of import licences to traditional, established importers could assure existing exporters of duty-free entry for a certain proportion of their trade; but it 'froze' the structure of trade and discouraged new entrants. Given the overall constraint of a tariff quota, it is clear that no entirely satisfactory system could be found, and that uncertainties and anomalies would prevail.

Such restrictions and uncertainties cast considerable doubt on the real value of the scheme to developing countries. If importers could not be assured of duty-free treatment for the goods they purchased, the chance of a reduction in selling prices on the European market was slim: and thus ldc exporters could not benefit from the increase in demand which would follow from greater price competitiveness. Thus in sensitive products limited by tariff quotas, little trade creation was likely. However, the fact that importers could make extra profits from lower import prices, even for part of their trade, might induce them to divert some of their purchases to new preferential sources of supply, and away from non-EEC developed countries where these were main alternative sources of imports. Again, trade diversion rather than trade creation was likely to be the major consequence of the Community scheme.

The GSP in Practice – Wider Reactions

Many of the problems foreseen in principle by UNCTAD and other critics, and many 'teething troubles' connected with the practical operation of the GSP – such as those connected with the operation of the internationally agreed and coordinated origin certificate system on which GSP access depends in practice – emerged within the first year of operation of the schemes. It also became clear that one of the biggest practical difficulties in operating the network of GSP schemes was that of informing and educating administrators in potential beneficiary countries on the operation of the various schemes and on how best to take advantage of them.

To this end, UNCTAD, as an executive agency for UNDP, in cooperation with regional organisations of the UN, promoted a three-year training and advisory project on implementation of the GSP. A series of seminars for ldc trade and customs officials were held between September 1972 and November 1973 in Beirut,[3] Santiago,[4] Addis Ababa,[5] Bangkok[6] and Brasilia.[7] It is to the credit of the EEC Commission that a strong team of officials closely concerned with the design and operation of the GSP attended each of the seminars (apart from the first in Beirut) and took considerable trouble to explain the operation of the Community scheme. It was obvious that the extent to which specific developing countries were able, or ready, to take advantage of GSP varied enormously. Most of the 'least developed' countries could derive relatively little benefit from any of the schemes since processed products were generally poorly covered (particularly in the Community scheme) and the EEC scheme also specifically ruled out semi-processed minerals and metals; and since a large proportion of the primary products exported by these countries are given mfn duty-free treatment the potential for preferences is, in any case, low. Many African countries were not directly interested in GSP access, in the absence of US and Canadian schemes (a major shortcoming of the GSP network), relying rather on the relatively unrestricted preferential duty-free access from which they benefited in the EEC or British markets. Indeed, the Yaoundé Associates took the opportunity to reiterate their fears that EEC preferences extended to them under Association would be seriously eroded by the GSP. The main positive impact of the GSP on ldcs' exports was seen as the degree of incentive it might provide to diversify trade into 'non-sensitive' manufactured goods, to undertake better market research and export promotion, and to reorganise their trade policies in a more export-oriented vein.

Generally, the more developed ldcs were in the best position to take advantage of GSP possibilities to promote exports. For example, among the Latin American and Caribbean countries represented at the Santiago seminar, eleven countries (Argentina, Brazil, Colombia, Dominican Republic, Ecuador, Guatemala, Honduras, Mexico, Peru, Uruguay, and Venezuela) had, by October 1972, been able to comply with all the origin and other administrative requirements of existing GSP schemes, 'and, in so doing, had encountered very few problems'.[8] But the GSP had not significantly diversified their export markets or the structure of trade, nor led to any significant expansion of non-traditional exports, even in the four countries which had already undertaken special studies of GSP prospects for exporters.[9]

A second group of nine countries (Bolivia, Chile, Costa Rica, Cuba, Jamaica, Nicaragua, Panama, Paraguay, Trinidad) had taken little advantage of GSP concessions, for three main reasons: first, most of them were highly dependent on the export of primary commodities which were either covered by international commodity arrangements (e.g. coffee) or faced major non-tariff barriers in developed countries (e.g. sugar); second, the productive capacities of many of their emerging industries was thought inadequate to cope with large increases in exports; third, most of their non-primary exports were adequately taken up within the region. Only a few products were exported under GSP terms: and, significantly, the main pressure to trade within the GSP had come from importers, rather than from exporters.

A third group (Barbados, El Salvador, Haiti, and Guyana) had taken virtually no action. Either their exportable 'non-traditional' products did not qualify, under value-added criteria of origin, or their commercial infrastructure appeared inadequate to cope with the complications of the system. These were seen as, principally, the ways in which EEC tariff quotas were administered, the rules of origin, particularly the lack of 'cumulative origin' provisions, the variety of different schemes applied by different developed countries, language problems (for Spanish- and

Portuguese-speaking countries) and the difficulties of obtaining acceptable transit certificates for exports from land-locked countries.

Many of the criticisms of the network of GSP schemes, and particularly of the Community's highly complex system, appear to have been borne out in practice, at least initially. Important trading gains may well have been made by countries which can – through initiatives from either the exporting or importing side – organise their trade to promote exports of non-sensitive products, or whose exports are low enough in value to avoid *butoir* limits. But overall, the scheme is likely to divert, rather than increase, trade. On the global scale, the continuing lack of US and Canadian schemes has been a serious handicap, on the one hand, to many ldcs whose exports are biased in those directions, and, on the other, to a greater willingness among other developed countries to improve their own schemes.

Improvements in the Community scheme

The Commission must be given credit for having been sensitive to criticism of the GSP. But any improvements which have been made since 1971 have been strongly contested: and scope for improving the scheme has continued to be limited by the prior claims of Association and the attitudes of the member states. It is true that the terms for processed agricultural goods have been gradually improved. The list has been enlarged, particularly in 1974 when 57 products including cocoa butter, vegetable oils and fats, soluble coffee and fishmeal were added, and the general preferential tariff reduction increased from 20 per cent to 40 per cent of mfn duties. Further improvements proposed for 1975 (preferential margin increased to 50 per cent, some new additions to the list) are noted in Chapter 9. UNCTAD noted that the 1974 scheme covered 10 per cent of dutiable imports in BTN chapters 1-24, as against under 2 per cent in the original scheme.[10] But this is still a small proportion, and the margins of preference proposed even for 1975 still fall far short of the duty-free entry extended by Britain and Denmark before 1974.

Similarly, up to 1974, most competing manufactures were on the 'sensitive' list and hence subject to the most restrictive forms of tariff quota. Some reductions were made in the list in 1974. As Table 8.3 shows, only a few of the overall tariff quotas were being filled. Most were seriously under-used except by a few highly competitive countries (particularly Hong Kong, Yugoslavia and South Korea) whose exports consistently reached *butoir* levels. The complexity of the 'sensitive' tariff quota system was a frequent bone of contention which had been heavily criticised in UNCTAD secretariat studies. Proposals for the 1975 GSP suggested, therefore, that the large majority (44 out of 51) of 'sensitive' non-textile products could be transferred to the less rigid surveillance of the semi-sensitive list where normally *butoirs* would be 50 per cent and the overall tariff quota would not be pre-allocated among the Nine in the arbitrary manner which had hitherto been such a bone of contention. The only goods which would remain 'sensitive' outside the textile group would be some fertilizers, vulcanised fibre, plywood and blockboard (where a special tariff quota had in any case been brought in for British imports from Malaysia), footwear and electronic goods. At the same time, however, countries which had hit the *butoir* level on the 44 products now regarded as semi-sensitive (which included nitrogenous fertilisers, travel goods, leather clothing, umbrellas, china and glassware, sewing machines, binoculars, record players and tapedecks, furniture, and dolls and toys) would be limited to the 1974 *butoir* level, or to 15 per cent of the overall tariff quota, whichever was the greater. Countries whose *per capita* GNP was under $ 275 per annum or which were heavily dependent on these products among their industrial exports might be relieved from this provision.

If this provision is brought into effect in 1975, it would no doubt limit the most competitive countries. But would it necessarily help the others? It would, at least in principle, if the same products were on offer from other sources. The UNCTAD Secretariat, however, was pessimistic about the way the system had worked up to 1973:

> 'Despite the low maximum amount limitations, only exceptionally was more than one beneficiary affected . . . The data seem to suggest that the products subject to certain tariff quotas have been narrowly defined with the purpose of limiting preferential imports from preferential suppliers. In fact, in a number of cases after application of the maximum amount limitation there were practically no other beneficiaries capable of utilising the remaining part of the quota. Thus far from achieving its declared objective of ensuring preferential advantages to less competitive beneficiary suppliers, the maximum amount limitation by and large results in a sterilization of trade over and above that caused by the single allocation to each member state.'[11]

Table 8.3

1972 Products on which the Common External Tariff was re-imposed under the EEC GSP 'ceiling' system

BTN Number	Product	Countries	Date
56.05 A	Yarn of discontinuous synthetic	All	26. 1.72
71.16	Artificial jewellery	Hong Kong[2]	16. 2.72
62.02	Bedlinen etc., of cotton	India	16. 2.72
60.03 (ex)	Socks, etc., not of cotton	S. Korea	26. 2.72
42.03 B 1	Protective gloves	Hong Kong	2. 3.72
97.02	Dolls	Hong Kong	2. 3.72
64.02 A	Footwear, leather uppers	Yugoslavia	2. 3.72
61.01 (ex)	Men's and boys' outergarments, not of cotton	S. Korea	3. 3.72
61.03 (ex)	Men's and boy's undergarments[1]	S. Korea	3. 3.72
54.03	Flax or ramie yarn	All	3.72
7012	Glass inners for vacuum flasks	Yugoslavia	18. 3.72
87.14 B II	Trainers and semi-trailers	Yugoslavia	18. 3.72
42.02 A	Travel goods, of plastic	Hong Kong	27. 3.72
B	Other	Kong Kong	29. 3.72
55.09 A II (ex)	Cotton fabrics, 115-165 cm, wide	S. Korea	2. 4.72
76.03	Wrought plates, sheet and strip of aluminium	Yugoslavia	13. 4.72
46.03	Basket work etc.	Philippines	14. 4.72
69.02	Refractory bricks, etc.	Yugoslavia	14. 4.72
97.03	Toys and working models	Hong Kong	14. 4.72
60.05 A ex II	Knitted or crocheted outergarments	S. Korea	14. 4.72
42.03	Leather clothing and accessories	Yugoslavia	21. 4.72
85.21 D, E	Biodes, transistors and parts	Singapore	21. 4.72
31.05 A, B	'Other' fertilisers	Colombia	26. 4.72
61.05	Cotton handkerchiefs	S. Korea	17. 4.72
61.01	Men's and boy's cotton outergarments[1]	S. Korea	
97.05	Carnival articles, tricks, jokes	Hong Kong	28. 4.72
85.10 B	Torches and battery lamps, other	Hong Kong	29. 4.72
58.01 A	Carpets, knotted, over 350 rows	Iran	29. 4.72
31.05	'Other' fertilisers	Yugoslavia	30. 4.72
61.02	Women's and girl's cotton outer-garments[1]	India	2. 5.72
46.03	Basket and wickerwork	Yugoslavia	6. 5.72
66.01	Umbrellas, etc.	Hong Kong	13. 5.72
67.04	Wigs, hairpieces	Hong Kong	13. 5.72
39.03 B II	Cellulose nitrates	Yugoslavia	17. 5.72
60.05 A ex II ex B	Knitted garments	All	19. 5.72
85.01 A II	'Other' generators and motors	Yugoslavia	23. 5.72
85.15 AIII CIII	Radio and TV receivers and parts	Hong Kong	23. 5.72
62.02	Bedlinen etc., of cotton	Pakistan	23. 5.72
83.01	Locks etc.	Hong Kong	27. 5.72
55.05 BII	Cotton yarn	Colombia	29. 5.72
70.05	Drawn or blown glass[1]	Yugoslavia	30. 5.72
94.01 B	'Other' chairs and seats	Yugoslavia	31. 5.72

BTN Number	Product	Countries	Date
79.03 A	Wrought plates etc., of zinc	Yugoslavia	3. 6.72
87.12	Parts of bicycles	Yugoslavia	3. 6.72
90.05	Telescopes and binoculars	Macao	3. 6.72
55.09 A II	'Other' cotton fabrics	India	3. 6.72
50.09	Silk fabrics[1]	India	5. 6.72
85.04 A	Lead-acid accumulators[1]	Yugoslavia	6. 6.72
58.01 B	Silk carpets or rugs	Iran	6. 6.72
67.04	Wigs, hairpieces	S. Korea	9. 6.72
90.05	Telescopes and binoculars	S. Korea	9. 6.72
58.01 A	Woollen carpets, 350-500 knots per metre	Iran	9. 6.72
28.10	Phosphorous pentoxide, acids[1]	All	13. 6.72
85.23	Insulated electric wire	Yugoslavia	13. 6.72
95.03	Worked ivory and articles[1]	Hong Kong	13. 6.72
55.05 B II	Cotton yarn	Pakistan	16. 6.72
87.14 B II	Trailers and semi-trailers	All	17. 6.72
69.11	Porcelain and china ware	Macao	20. 6.72
85.21 D, E	Transistors and parts	Kong Kong	21. 6.72
28.27	Lead oxides	Mexico	24. 6.72
41.05 B II	Leather	Yugoslavia	27. 6.72
48.09	Building board[1]	Brazil	27. 6.72
61.01	Men's and boy's outergarments[1]	All	27. 6.72
61.02	Women's and girls' outergarments[1]	All	27. 6.72
61.03	Men's and boys' undergarments[1]	All	27. 6.72
97.06 B, C	Tennis rackets, 'other' sports equipment	Pakistan	2. 7.72
61.05	Handkerchiefs, cotton[1]	All	3. 7.72
91.09	Watch cases	Hong Kong	4. 7.72
94.03	Furniture	Yugoslavia	4. 7.72
55.09 A II	Calico	India	4. 7.72
62.03 B II	Sacks and bags, of cotton[1]	India	4. 7.72
56.07 A	Woven synthetic fabrics discontinuous	S. Korea	4. 7.72
55.05 B II	Cotton yarn	Colombia	12. 7.72
part 61.03	Men's and boys' cotton undergarments[1]	India	17. 7.72
70.14 B	Illuminating glassware	Kong Kong	22. 7.72
74.07 B	Copper tubes and pipes	Yugoslavia	29. 7.72
part 61.02	Women's and girls' outgarments other than cotton	S. Korea	30. 7.72
48.09	Building board[1]	All	14. 8.72
67.02	Artificial flowers[1]	Hong Kong	14. 8.72
44.14	Sawn sheets of wood	Brazil	11. 9.72
41.05 B II	'Other' leather[1]	All	30. 9.72
70.12	Vacuum flask liners[1]	All	30. 9.72
85.04 A	Lead-acid accumulators[1]	All	30. 8.72
85.19 B	Resistors	Brazil	30. 9.72
66.03	Parts of umbrellas etc.[1]	All	1.10.72
41.02	Bovine leather	Argentina	7.10.72
73.18	Iron and steel tubes	Yugoslavia	7.10.72
part 55.05 B II	Cotton yarn	U.A.R.	14.10.72
55.09 A II	Calico	U.A.R.	14.10.72
85.03	Primary cells and batteries	Hong Kong	17.10.72

BTN Number	Product	Countries	Date
58.01 B	Silk and synthetics carpets[1]	All	22.10.72
69.08	Tiles[1]	S. Korea	23.10.72
70.14 A II	Electric lighting equipment	Yugoslavia	30.10.72
part 55.05 B II	Cotton yarn	U.A.R.	30.10.72
85.15 A III CIII	Radio, TV receivers parts	Singapore	31.10.72
53.06	Wool for retail sale[1]	All	7.11.72
85.20	Electric light bulbs	Hong Kong	10.11.72
84.41 A	Sewing machines	S. Korea	14.12.72
82.09	Knives[1]	Hong Kong	18.11.72
82.14	Stainless steel cutlery[1]	Hong Kong	18.11.72
85.01 C	Parts for generators	Yugoslavia	20.11.72
part 59.04	Twine, rope, of hemp	Yugoslavia	27.11.72
28.19	Zinc oxide and peroxide[1]	Yugoslavia	22.12.72
97.04	Games equipment[1]	Hong Kong	25.12.72
68.12	Asbestos cement goods[1]	Yugoslavia	26.12.72

1. Not 'sensitive' products.

Source: *Trade and Industry*, HMSO

Table 8.4 shows the pattern of imports from ldcs to the Six of the goods likely to be affected by these provisions. The principal ldc supplier, in most cases, would be subject to the new *butoirs*. Most products were, in 1972, imported from more than one ldc, although the same names crop up again and again. It is therefore possible that trade may be directed from the most important ldc supplier to others. But the effect is most likely to be simply one of 'beggar-my-neighbour'. No new, or additional, trade is likely to be created by the limitation of duty-free access from the largest ldc suppliers, although the less complex 'semi-sensitive' regulations may have some beneficial effect.

What does, above all, stand out is the small share of EEC imports in most of these products accounted for by ldcs. Gloves, umbrellas, wigs, dolls, calcium carbide and lead oxide were the only goods where the most important ldc's share was over 10%. One must at least question the rationale for protecting Community producers against so small a threat to their stability.

TABLE 8.4

Main Products on Which 15% Butoir is Proposed for 1975

Product	Main ldc suppliers in in order of importance, 1972	Principal ldc's share (%) of total EEC (6) imports, 1972
Lead oxides	Mexico, Yugoslavia	15.3
Calcium carbide	Yugoslavia	22.2
Cellulose nitrates	Yugoslavia	7.4
Rubber tyres and tubes	Yugoslavia, Israel, Algeria, Panama.	0.5
Plastic travel goods	Hong Kong, Taiwan, Yugoslavia, S. Korea	7.4
Other travel goods	Hong Kong, Lebanon, Morocco, Yugoslavia	4.9
Protective gloves	Hong Kong, Taiwan, Pakistan	57.9
Sports gloves	Pakistan, Taiwan	20.5
'Other' clothing	Hong Kong, Brazil	2.4
Basketwork, etc.	Philippines, Yugoslavia, Hong Kong	10.8
'Other' Kraft paper	Yugoslavia	0.8
Umbrellas	Hong Kong, Taiwan, S. Korea, Singapore	25.4
Wigs	S. Korea, Hong Kong, Singapore, Taiwan	36.6
Refractory bricks, etc.	Yugoslavia, Israel	5.1
Porcelain ware	Macao, Hong Kong	0.1
Glass, rectangles	Yugoslavia, Turkey	1.7
Glassware	Yugoslavia, Turkey, Taiwan, Hong Kong	1.0
Tape and recorded players	Taiwan, Hong Kong, South Korea, Singapore	0.7
Chairs	Yugoslavia, Brazil, Egypt, Taiwan	3.9
Other furniture	Yugoslavia, Israel, Hong Kong, Brazil	1.3
Dolls	Hong Kong, Taiwan, South Korea	26.3
Other toys	Hong Kong, Taiwan, South Korea, Israel	6.6
Jokes, tricks, etc.	Hong Kong, Taiwan	2.6

Source: *EEC Statistics (NIMEXE) 1972.*

NOTES

1. Some tariff items are partly included in and partly excluded from the scheme. 'Max' figures assume that all such products are included: 'Min' figures, that all such are excluded. Presumably the 'true' coverage lies between the two extremes.
2. Yarn of discontinuous synthetic fibre, flax and ramie yarn, knitted garments, phosphorous pentoxide, trailers, men's and boys' outer and under garments, women's and girls' outer garments, cotton handkerchiefs, building board, 'other' leather, vacuum flask liners, lead-acid accumulators, parts of umbrellas, silk and synthetic carpets, wool for retail sale.
3. Attended by officials from Bahrein, Cyprus, Iraq, Jordan, Lebanon, Malta Saudi Arabia, Syria, Spain, Turkey, Yugoslavia.
4. Attended by officials from Argentina, Barbados, Bolivia, Brazil, Chile, Colombia, Costa Rica, Cuba, Dominican Republic, Ecuador, El Salvador, Guatemala, Guyana, Haiti, Honduras, Jamaica, Mexico, Nicaragua, Panama, Paraguay, Peru, Trinidad & Tobago, Uruguay, Venezuela.
5. Two seminars were held in Addis Ababa: the first for the African countries classified by the UN as 'least developed' or 'land-locked' (Burundi, Central African Republic, Dahomey, Ethiopia, Malawi, Mali, Sierra Leone, Sudan, Swaziland, Tanzania, Togo, Uganda, Upper Volta, Zambia) and the second for other African countries.
6. Attended by officials from Afghanistan, Bangladesh, Fiji, Hong Kong, India, Indonesia, Iran, Khmer Republic, South Korea, Malaysia, Nepal, Pakistan, Philippines, Singapore, Sri Lanka, Thailand, Western Samoa.
7. Attended by officials from Argentina, Brazil, Bulgaria, Colombia, Cyprus, Egypt, India, Israel, Indonesia, Kenya, Lebanon, South Korea, Malta, Mexico, Nigeria, Pakistan, Philippines, Romania, Singapore, Spain, Turkey, Uruguay, Yugoslavia, Hong Kong.
8. UNCTAD Document UNCTAD/TAP/41, November 1972, *Report of the Second Seminar on the GSP, organised by UNCTAD and ECLA,* p.21
9. Argentina, Ecuador, Guatemala and Uruguay.
10. UNCTAD TD/B/C.5 22, Second General Report on the Implementation of the Generalised System of Preferences, p.19.
11. *Op. cit.* Paras 121-122.

9. THE GSP IN COMMUNITY POLICY

We have seen how the Community's preference scheme developed historically. Some of the sources of pressure on its designers, and the directions in which these pressures moved Community thinking on the scheme, have been reviewed. But how does the GSP scheme now feature as an element of Community policy, and what difference has it made to the way in which policies towards developing countries are conducted by the Community?

On its own, the scheme is a small step towards greater Community control of trade policy; an acceptance of a new principle in an area, tariff policy, which was from the start regarded as a Community responsibility and which is fundamental to the customs union on which the Community is based. No areas of trade policy other than the Common External Tariff were affected directly by the development of the GSP. It is true that common policies are gradually evolving in other aspects of trade, for example import quotas (where member states have agreed on basic 'liberalised' lists where no import quotas are imposed by any member state, and where members are required to inform their Community partners if any new ones are introduced), health and safety regulations (gradually becoming coordinated as part of the general movement towards complete internal free trade) and some bilateral 'voluntary' export restraint agreements (such as any new agreements concluded under the GATT Multifibre Textile Arrangement). But these are quite separate from, and unaffected by, the GSP.

The GSP has helped to move the Community's *development* policy away from its heavy concentration on the special relationship between the EEC and the African ex-colonies. Firstly, its existence helped to ease the path of entry to the Community for Britain by ensuring that Asian Commonwealth countries would, at least to some degree, continue to benefit from duty-free entry to the British market after 1973.[1] Moreover, many of the changes made in the enlarged Community's scheme for 1974 and 1975 were intended to be for the benefit of this group, in the spirit of the Joint Declaration of Intent written into the 1972 Treaty of Accession.[2]

Secondly, since Community enlargement development policy has been under continuous review. The 1972 Summit meeting of Community political leaders held in Paris called on the Community to adopt 'an overall policy of development cooperation on a world-wide scale.'[3] GSP improvement was to be one of the main planks of this policy. At the same time, priority was still to be attached to the maintenance of Association; and during 1973 and 1974 the Community was negotiating with the original Yaoundé Associates, Commonwealth African, Caribbean and Pacific countries, and three non-Commonwealth countries in Africa (Ethiopia, Liberia and the Sudan) for a new convention of association. And from April 1974 onwards, the Labour government in Britain sought changes in Community development policies as part of the 'renegotiation package' which it had promised to undertake on election.

Within the Commission, too, there appears to be a more open attitude overall to a 'world-wide' development policy. The effects of the oil 'crisis' on some developing countries, and not simply on Associates, have focussed the Commission's attention on emergency aid to the hardest-hit countries, including India and Bangladesh. Changes in Community personnel – particularly the appointment of Mr Claude Cheysson at the head of DG VIII – and the wider brief given to DG VIII since Community enlargement have helped to bring about this change in attitude.

Lastly, the GSP is one important trade policy factor which has to be taken into account by the EEC and its trading partners in planning a negotiating strategy for a new round of GATT trade negotiations, inaugurated formally in September 1973 in Tokyo but held up throughout 1974 by the lack of a negotiating mandate for the United States. This aspect will be covered in the following chapter. In this chapter, we are concerned with the GSP as an aspect of the Community's changing, but still piecemeal, development policies.

The Enlarged Community and the 'Harmonised' GSP

Under Protocol 23 of the Treaty of Accession, the British and Danish governments agreed to bring their own GSP schemes, previously independent, into line with that of the Six:

> 'The new Member States are authorised to defer until 1 January 1974 the application of the generalised tariff preference scheme applied by the European Economic Community to products originating in the developing countries.'

From the wording of the protocol, there is no doubt what was intended – that Britain and Denmark should give up their existing preference schemes and adopt the same system as all the other member states. For both new members this meant a change in the type of system which they would apply. The schemes which Britain and Denmark had introduced in January 1972 were of the 'safeguard clause with exceptions' type rejected by the Six. Specific ranges of manufactured goods were expressly ruled out of GSP access, while an escape clause, under which duties could be re-applied to products in case of market disruption, was built into the provisions for those included. The British scheme had specifically excluded cotton and competing synthetic textiles, hydrocarbon oils, perfumes, matches and lighters. Denmark's scheme had included all BTN 25-99 products but had ruled dependent territories out of its coverage as far as textiles, clothing and footwear was concerned – as in the EEC scheme, with the intention of excluding Hong Kong from preferences on these goods. Britain had extended duty-free access to manufactures and processed agricultural goods; Denmark had given duty-free access on some agricultural products, but not the majority.

Although Britain (if not Denmark) had accepted from the signature of the Treaty of Accession that the form of the enlarged Community's GSP would be that of the scheme operated by the Six, it was widely understood that an overall review of the scheme would be undertaken during 1973 with the aim of making some major improvements in it, as the communiqué of the October 1972 'Summit' had suggested. This review, carried out by a high-level committee of national and Community officials, resulted in the 1974 scheme outlined in Chapter 2, which incorporated a new base year for tariff quotas, a small number of improvements in the coverage of processed agricultural goods and some special concessions to British and Commonwealth Asian interests.

Once again, the question of how to treat processed agricultural goods was the hardest fought issue in the 'improvement' debate; and the outcome was much less of an improvement than Commission protagonists of the GSP had hoped.[4] Although the high level committee's initial report on a 'world-wide development policy', submitted to the Council in June 1973, included proposals for improving the GSP, and although the Commission had put up proposals for new provisions on processed agricultural goods as early as July, the whole scheme for 1974 was not finally approved by the Council until the last minute – the Council meeting on 5-6 December 1973; and neither was duty-free access given on processed goods nor was the list expanded as far as the Commission and the more liberal member states had hoped.

Association Policy and the GSP

It was seen in Chapter 7 that the interests of the original Yaoundé Associates of the Community, whose Association Convention was renewed in 1969, influenced Community thinking on the GSP considerably. Association was, for the Six (and particularly for France and Belgium), a priority commitment to which other aspects of development policy, like the GSP, should be subordinated.

The 1973 review of Community policy had once again to reconcile the apparently conflicting interests of Association with the creation of a more broadly based development policy. Under the provisions of Protocol 22 of the Treaty of Accession, Commonwealth African, Caribbean and Pacific countries were entitled to seek association with the Community on the same terms as Yaoundé Convention members. The negotiations have since been widened to include all independent Sub-Saharan African developing countries. The association negotiations might have created serious new entrenched interests against more liberal treatment for non-associates. The Community's commitment to the association negotiations meant that, if a more 'global' attitude towards development policy were to be encouraged, any new association agreement would have to be as flexible as possible.

Faced with the need to fulfil the twin mandate handed down by the 1972 summit, Jean-Francois Deniau, the Commissioner for Development Cooperation until April 1973, argued tenaciously that its two aims were not in conflict. This view was developed during 1973 by officials of DG VIII. By the end of the year their 'corporate view' under the new Commissioner Cheysson appeared to be something like this: that the issues of association and other development policies were most conveniently dealt with if kept separate, as far as possible; and that although the negotiation and enlargement of Association was politically the first priority, other matters – such as, for example, the development (through GSP and other concessions) of better trading conditions for the 'Joint Declaration of Intent' countries of the Asian Commonwealth – could be pursued at the same time and as far as possible without coming into conflict with the aims of association. Some DG VIII officials also developed the view that an approach to development policy which moved from a base in Association outwards, step by step, to create a wider development policy based on separate, rather specific agreements with different groups of ldcs was not only a desirable approach, but the only possible one in the face of the Community's own divisions on relations with the Third World. These rather cautious views reflected real, and deep, divisions at all three levels – among the member states, within the Commission, and among the Associates and Associables themselves – on the importance and permanence of Association *vis-a-vis* other aspects of development policy.

The negotiations for the enlargement of association opened formally in July 1973, and got under way in October, after the summer break. The aim was to sign a new association convention, if possible with all 44 developing countries involved, in time to come into force on 1 February 1975.

Initially it appeared that the ACP states,[5] although negotiating as one group under the eyes, in the Africans' case, of the Organisation for African Unity, would be divided along Yaoundé versus non-Yaoundé lines. The main issues on which such a division might have appeared were those of reciprocity ('reverse' preferences for Community products) and the permanence of a special preferential connection between 'Europe' and 'Africa'. The more Francophile of the Francophone states, in particular Senegal under President Senghor, attached considerable importance to reciprocity, as symbolizing political equality between the Community and its less-developed partners. Other ACP countries, following the lead given by UNCTAD, rejected the idea of reciprocity. On its side, the Commission, speaking for the Community did its best to defuse the 'reverse preferences' issue in advance by stressing, in its initial memorandum,[6] that reciprocity did not necessarily mean giving EEC exports better treatment than other countries' goods. But the Commission took the line, for much of the first year of the negotiations, that it was important to base any new association on a free trade area. This was mainly in order to preserve the permanent, contractual relationship which, it was argued, was involved in Association (as distinct from policies such as the GSP which were 'determined largely on the basis of autonomous decisions taken by the Community itself'.[7]

The Community's main fear was that abolishing the reciprocal element of Association would nullify the legal fiction of a free trade area, involving tariff-free access on both sides for 'substantially all' trade, under which Association was justified in the General Agreement on Tariffs and Trade (GATT).[8] If this fell, it was argued, the EEC and its Associates would probably have to apply for a special waiver of GATT rules to give preferences for Associates international legal validity. Such a waiver – probably, in effect, a new modification of the most-favoured nation provision of GATT Article I – would require a unanimous vote of all the contracting parties and would also have to be re-examined from time to time. Even if only one country which objected to special preferences for Associates voted against, the waiver would fall. It was thought unlikely that no such objection would ever occur, for example from the United States or – perhaps more likely – from some non-associated ldc.

However, up till the present the United States' main apparent objection to the Association has been to the existence of 'reverse' preferences by Associates for Community products and the advantages which these have conferred on Community exporters and investors. Moreover, the ACP countries appeared to be on reasonably strong ground, even in GATT terms, in arguing for non-reciprocity. This principle had been written into the General Agreement in Part IV, Article XXXVI:

> 'The developed contracting parties do not expect reciprocity for commitments made by them in trade negotiations to reduce or remove tariffs and other barriers to the trade of less-developed contracting parties.'

(But a note to this section made it clear that the phrase 'do not expect reciprocity' meant that ldcs should not have to 'make contributions which are inconsistent with their individual development, financial and trade needs' – not that they should make no return concessions at all.)

Agreement on the principle of non-reciprocity in the new Association was reached in a Ministerial Conference held in Kingston, Jamaica, on 25-26 July 1974:

> 'As regards trade arrangements, the participants recognised that the keynote should be stability and recognition of the fact that the developing countries are in an unequal position *vis-a-vis* their partners. The main feature of these arrangements will be free access for the ACP States to the Community market, no corresponding commitments being required of the ACP States.'[9]

As with the previous Association convention, there appears to be no express commitment to giving Associates generally better tariff treatment than that given to other ldcs under the GSP. The three areas in which Association can be seen as conferring some special advantage are, firstly the treatment of Associates' primary products (for which a special export revenue stabilisation scheme is proposed); secondly, the treatment of CAP products (where the ACP group is pressing for free access and the Community *is* at least committed to giving better treatment than that extended to other ldcs); and thirdly, 'industrial cooperation' between the Community and its Associates.

The combination of an export revenue stabilisation scheme and aid for industrial cooperation, for Associates, was seen by the Commission as offsetting any cut in the preferential terms given to Associates which might result from bringing more processed agricultural goods into the GSP. Processed goods were, in 1974 as in 1969, the main sensitive area, as far as Associates were concerned. In its proposals for 1975, the Commission suggested that new improvements could be made in this area of the GSP, firstly because the safeguard clause had never been applied – largely because the 'preferential' tariff cuts on processed agricultural goods were too small to encourage any trade) and secondly because of the new stabilisation scheme to be built into the proposed association convention. In general, it was suggested that preferential margins on processed agricultural goods should be 50 per cent of mfn rates for 1975, and that duties of 5 per cent or lower should be abolished. Some new products – honey, orchids, anchovies, tapioca substitutes – should be added. On products which competed directly with the Associates' exports, small concessions might be made to non-associates under specific conditions. The provisions for Virginia tobacco from India, introduced in 1974, would be extended for a further year and a tonnage, rather than value, tariff quota introduced in order to safeguard a specific quantity of exports. Palm oil, palm kernel oil, coconut oil for human consumption, and pepper should be brought into the GSP scheme when the new Association convention came into effect. The GSP duty on pepper should be 8 per cent (80 per cent of the mfn level) as against duty-free access for Associates: and duties on vegetable oils (between 5 and 20 per cent at mfn rates) should be changed into 'specific' duties levied on the unit of quantity, so that effective protection would be low when prices were high and high when prices were low.

At the time of writing (August 1974) the Council had not considered the Commission's proposals. But although there still appears to be an effort to maintain special advantages for Associates from 1975 onwards – particularly through the proposals for an export revenue stabilisation scheme and by giving better access for CAP products from Associates – the distinct hierarchical division between the two groups of ldcs is gradually becoming blurred.

Separate Tables – the Community and Groups of LDCs

Since enlargement, the Community's development policy has operated along several separate lines. The enlargement of Association is one. The creation of a common Mediterranean policy is another. The development of relations with India and Bangladesh through special trade and cooperation agreements (still in their infancy) is a third. A fourth, new line of action, still unexplored, may follow the Council's acceptance in principle, in July 1974, that joint Community aid, possibly parallel to that given through the European Development Fund to Associates, should be extended to other ldcs. And this is again separate from the proposal made in 1974 by Commissioner Cheysson that the Community should contribute $ 500m. to a special emergency fund of $ 3,000m. in all, half to be contributed by OECD countries[11] and half by the Arab oil exporters, to help the developing countries hardest hit by the quadrupling in the price of oil between 1973 and 1974.[12] In addition, the Community has a variety of trade agreements, usually non-preferential and rather restricted in scope, with various Asian and Latin American ldcs (Thailand, Philippines, Indonesia, Sri Lanka, Argentina, Uruguay, and Brazil). Are these separate lines likely to become a coherent development policy? And what might this look like?

In these early days of the enlarged Community, only speculation is possible. But the history of EEC decision-making is not one of dramatic new departures and reversals of policy, and even 'renegotiation' is likely to build on and expand existing policies. And the future direction of policy will once again depend greatly on the direction and strength of pressure by Community members. So far, a few clear signposts exist. A new Association convention will, barring accidents, be concluded. British policy makers appear satisfied with the degree of unity shown by the ACP states and, as long as the question of Caribbean sugar exports can be settled, will probably be happy to see the new convention come into force. Agreement on a common policy towards North African and Mediterranean island states has been reached at least in principle among the Nine. If Britain is willing to support the efforts being made by India, Bangladesh and the five ASEAN countries (Indonesia, Malaysia, Philippines, Singapore, Thailand) to get favourable terms within trade and cooperation agreements with the Community, these will stand a better chance of success. The Commission has made a helpful move towards ASEAN, as well as to the Andean Group [13] and the Central American Common Market, by proposing that a cumulative system of rules of origin should be brought into the GSP for 1975 so that goods using materials from two or more countries within the groups can qualify for GSP terms. This is one measure which the Council of Ministers should, as a minimum, support.

It will be interesting to see what becomes of the proposal to give Community aid to non-associables. Although the principle was established in 1974, no figure is likely to be settled at least until a new EDF total is decided upon for the new Association convention. The British government proposed during 1974 that Community aid should be divided equally between Associates and other ldcs; but no more specific proposals were made and the British suggestion was not discussed before the summer break. It must be counted unlikely that the British proposal will be accepted by the Council without reservation. But whatever total is determined, criteria for the allocation of aid among countries will be a crucial factor. The need criterion in this case coincides with the political interests of Britain and West Germany, in indicating a high proportion of any new Community aid for South and South East Asian countries.

It is likely, then, that the 'global' policy of the enlarged Community will still be rather less than world-wide. Africa, in the shape of the enlarged Association *plus* the Mediterranean group, is obviously still going to be an area of concentration. The Caribbean and Pacific islands will hang on Africa's coat-tails. Some parts of Asia will also be largely ignored, except insofar as they benefit from the GSP on manufacturers and can negotiate non-preferential trade agreements with the enlarged

EEC. Agriculture generally will still be a sore point, for Latin American exporters in particular.

NOTES

1. Detailed assessments of the effects of EEC enlargement on Commonwealth Asia are given in the Peter Tulloch, *The Seven Outside,* ODI, 1973, and Dharam Ghai, *Asian Commonwealth Countries and the EEC,* Commonwealth Secretariat, 1973.
2. Cmnd. 5179, January 1972, p. 281
3. Cmnd. 5199, October 1972.
4. Tran-Van-Thinh in *European Community,* January 1972, had suggested that since the treatment of processed agricultural goods in the British scheme was 'distinctly more advantageous' than that given by the Six, the British system of duty-free access might be adopted by the Nine. This proved, in the event, much too optimistic.
5. African, Caribbean and Pacific.
6. Com (73) 500/fin., 4 April 1973.
7. *Ibid.,* p.17.
8. Press Release issued at Kingston Conference, quoted in *Telex Africa,* Brussels, 30 July 1974, p. A4.
9. Press Release issued at Kingston Conference, quoted in *Telex Africa,* Brussels, 30 July 1974, p. A4.
10. In fact $ 500m. each from the Community, the United States, and Japan.
11. Including Bangladesh, India, Sri Lanka and many of the 'least developed' countries.
12. Bolivia, Chile, Colombia, Ecuador, Peru, Venezuela.

10. DEVELOPING COUNTRIES, THE GSP AND GATT

In September 1973, the international community formally inaugurated a new 'round' of negotiations aimed at reducing barriers to international trade. These negotiations are to take place under the aegis of GATT (the General Agreement on Tariffs and Trade); but they are to be open to any country which wishes to take part, whether or not a member of GATT.

By August 1974 no progress had been made, and indeed no real negotiations had taken place. The main reason was that the United States Administration had not been able to gain congressional approval for a Trade Bill which would enable the USA to take part in the negotiations. Without the USA, talks could not begin.

The negotiations, when they do begin, are intended to cover all aspects of trade, and all types of tariff and non-tariff barriers to trade. 83 countries are taking part, of which 55 are less developed countries which already benefit from GSP treatment in the Community and other major developed countries, but not in the USA and Canada. What role is the GSP likely to play in the negotiations, and what should ldcs attitudes to it be? Initially, while nothing happens in the GATT talks, most ldcs have an obvious interest in maximising their use of existing GSP concessions and in extending the scope of the system. But is the maintenance of limited preferential advantages, based on the strictest possible non-reciprocity, likely to be in ldcs' best interests in the long run; or might a more flexible attitude pay greater dividends?

Four areas of GATT negotiations are likely to be most important for developing countries. First, cuts in import duties on processed raw materials, whether agricultural or mineral. Second, a reduction in agricultural protection in developed countries, including CAP levies in the Community. Third, a general move to reduce non-tariff barriers, including effective international control of 'voluntary' export limitation agreements, on their exports to developed countries. Lastly, the introduction of GSP schemes by the USA and Canada. Most of these areas of negotiation do not directly involve the GSP, although cuts in tariffs on processed goods may be given on a preferential basis.

In turn, three areas of interest to the OECD developed countries were outlined in a report[2] presented to the Secretary General of OECD in August 1972. These were, first, sure and regular supplies of raw materials, for example though long-term contracts. (This must assume even greater importance in the aftermath of the oil supply crisis of

1973/4.) Second, reciprocal trade concessions in the form of reductions in tariff and non-tariff barriers, especially from 'countries that have already reached a certain level of development and have large markets'. A third suggestion was that ldcs should promote schemes aimed at encouraging investment 'arranged in such a way as to be equitable both to countries which receive and countries which supply investment.' And a fourth area where developed countries are likely to drive a hard bargain – if the example of the Multifibre Textile Arrangement signed in December 1973 sets a precedent – is that of internationally administered safeguards against 'market disruption' by imports from developing countries.

The principle of non-reciprocity for trade concessions given by developed to developing countries, which UNCTAD and the ldcs have fought so hard to promote, was not kindly treated in the Tokyo declaration with which the GATT negotiations were formally opened.[3] Although developing countries' interests were mentioned in practically every paragraph, the furthest the declaration would go was to say that 'The developed countries do not expect the developing countries, in the course of the trade negotiations, to make contributions which are inconsistent with their individual development, financial and trade needs'.[4] This extremely vague formula revealed developed countries' extreme reluctance to be seen 'giving away' concessions to the more competitive ldcs without any apparent possibility of gains in return.

In practice individuals and groups among ldcs clearly have different interests. The attempts by producers of minerals (e.g. bauxite, copper, iron ore) to form new production cartels or to strengthen existing agreements in order to keep raw material prices high reveal some of the interest groups. Ldcs which are not producers of such materials are, presumably, on the other side. Exporters of 'competing' agricultural products have different aims from those of tropical foods. In general, however, it is the poorest ldcs – the 25 'least developed' countries and perhaps those hardest hit by the 1974 oil crisis – who may be able to look for the most liberal treatment from developed countries. Others will probably have to give some reciprocal 'concessions'.

The Role of the GSP

Up to the end of 1973, during an initial position-taking phase in the embryonic negotiations, the effect of the GSP on developed countries' attitudes was mainly negative. Ldcs were concerned with bringing the USA and Canada into line with other developed countries. The United States, having failed to produce a GSP scheme in 1971, was once again using its 'offer' of a scheme as a bargaining counter, to play off against the abolition of reverse preferences within the EEC's Association policies. The Community was also using its scheme as part of a bargaining strategy aimed at preserving the Common External Tariff at some level, and hence maintaining an internal customs union with protection against outside suppliers. (Although, as we have seen in Chapter 1, the extension of a free trade area to other European countries reduced protection within the EEC for industrial goods considerably.) Overall, the Community proposed that tariff reductions should not go below a certain, unspecified level, while proportional cuts should be made on all tariffs. This would ensure that very high tariffs would fall more than moderate or low duties.

One justification given for this approach was that to cut customs tariffs on an mfn basis inevitably reduced the benefits which ldcs could derive from the GSP. The Community, therefore, reserved the right to propose that a small number of products included in the GSP, of particular interest to less-developed countries, should be excepted, specifically, from mfn tariffs cuts agreed in the negotiations.

The Community's attitude was, on the face of it, in line with that taken by many developed countries and by UNCTAD in wishing to maintain preferential terms for ldcs. But the UNCTAD Secretariat had already suggested, as has been noted,[5] that Western European countries were the main competitors faced by ldcs in GSP products. Since most of these countries are already, or will be soon, on free trade area terms with the Community, the argument against tariff cuts to maintain ldcs' preferences looks much less powerful.

Is the GSP a Side Issue?

The arguments for maintaining GSP terms cover only one class of trade barrier; tariffs on manufactures and a limited range of processed products. Over the years, developed countries' protection of processed goods produced domestically (particularly agriculture) through price supports, and the expanding range of non-tariff barriers they imposed, have become more and more important. It would be too simple to say that in all cases, as import duties fall, non-tariff restrictions rise; but it is likely that as more ldcs become competitive in more manufactures this will happen. How should ldcs approach these problems?

In processed products, the ldcs' approach may depend on where the problems actually lie. Their main handicap in this area may be that of competition primarily with domestic sources of supply in the EEC, American and Japanese markets rather than with other ldcs. If this is so, as the evidence of past EEC attitudes as to GSP concessions suggests, there may be more mileage to be gained by ldcs from striking genuine bargains than in seeking GSP 'concessions' which are visibly one-sided. This might be done by offering scope for investment in the development of processing industries in the relevant ldcs, with the aim of creating regular supplies to developed countries' markets, as a *quid pro quo* for tariff and quota-free access, on a most-favoured-nation basis.

As far as the use of 'safeguard clauses' by developed countries is concerned, the ldcs' main interest will, presumably, be in stopping the proliferation of unilateral, arbitrary 'market disruption' provisions applied by developed countries to competitive ldc exports, against which – since most exporting ldcs have less economic power than importers in the manufactures field – they have little redress. Ldcs may here be able to ally their own interests to those of certain of the major trading countries (particularly Japan) which may wish to avoid the escalation of 'safeguards' and thus of protection in general.

To be acceptable to the main developed importing countries, it must be possible to impose sanctions on particular products from particular sources of 'disruptive' imports. On the other hand, developing countries entering or enlarging export markets for manufactures and processed goods have a direct interest in seeing that their growing exports are not subject to arbitrary restriction in importing countries because of alleged 'market disruption'; nor forced into 'voluntary' export limitation agreements with no fixed term, as happened in many cases of ldcs' textile exports. So a multilaterally supervised safeguard clause, linked to adjustment programmes, is likely to appeal to them.

To date, the only area in which an international agreement on the use of safeguards has been negotiated is textiles. The new Multifibre Textile Arrangement (MTA), negotiated in GATT and signed in December 1973, does not set an encouraging precedent for developing countries.

The agreement covers substantially all classes of textiles and clothing except for those certified as 'handicraft' or 'cottage industry' products. Importing countries may, under Article 3, unilaterally limit imports of 'disruptive' products from particular sources (subject to consultation with the exporters) to the previous year's level, in the first year. Thereafter imports must be allowed to rise by a minimum annual rate of 6 per cent. Or importers may conclude 'voluntary' bilateral agreements with exporting countries to 'eliminate real risks of market disruption' while ensuring 'the expansion and orderly development of trade in textiles and the equitable treatment of participating countries' (Article 4). Existing quotas and 'voluntary' agreements can be retained as long as they are brought into line with the general provisions of the Arrangement (such as the 6 per cent annual growth rate). The definition of 'market disruption' used is loose: 'a sharp and substantial increase or *imminent increase* of imports of particular products from one particular source', offered at 'prices substantially below those prevailing for similar goods of comparable quality in the market of the importing country' – although the price comparison must, laudably, be with other imports as well as with domestic production. But developed countries can determine unilaterally what imports are disruptive.

Some safeguards for ldcs are built into the agreement. Their exports should, in principle, be more liberally treated (with higher basic quotas and annual minimum growth rates) than those from other countries; exports from new entrants to particular export markets should be allowed to grow more rapidly than past performance would indicate, and exports from countries whose total exports are small should not be restricted.

The whole arrangement is to be supervised by a small international jury (the Textiles Surveillance Body) set up under the GATT. Its sanctions are very weak. It must review any new quota arrangements or voluntary restrictions, and can recommend changes; but importing countries are under no obligation to follow its recommendations. Exporting countries may, however, appeal in the last resort to the GATT Ministerial Council if they are not satisfied with the state of affairs.

The growth rate provisions laid down are low compared to the actual growth of developed countries' textile imports from ldcs (estimated to average 23.7 per cent a year in current values in the period 1965-72, and accelerating in the later years). There are no time-related specific provisions for adjustment programmes in importing countries (although Article 1 provides that 'actions taken under this Arrangement *should be* accompanied by . . . appropriate economic and social policies . . . to encourage businesses which are less competitive internationally to move progressively into more viable lines of production or into other sectors of the economy, and provide increased access to their markets for imports from less-developed countries'). And the effectiveness of the international surveillance is likely to be small.

Nevertheless, the arrangement is probably a better deal for ldcs interested in exporting textiles than no international regulation, in the present protectionist climate. Without it a jungle of arbitrary regulations might arise. But its value depends on how strictly or liberally it is applied; and on past evidence, any ldc which becomes an effective competitor in textiles is likely to be hit hard. It is to be assumed that ldcs will, in the GATT negotiations, press the case vigorously for more effective international control and more liberal access terms in competing manufactures.

The Future of the GSP

The principal areas of the GATT negotiations in which ldcs may be interested are much wider than the GSP. The further development of GSP schemes depends, above all (and far too much) on the goodwill and altruism of developed countries' governments. Without any attempt at offsetting concessions by developing countries themselves, moral suasion becomes the only tool which ldcs can use to persuade the rich world to allow their goods entry into its markets. And it is not enough.

It is easy enough to say that it is to the advantage of consumers in the developed world to allow the freest possible entry for all types of products made or processed in developing countries; and no doubt, in terms of general welfare, this is so. But governments act generally in a short-term perspective (if only because four, five or seven years in office is the most that any government can expect) and in the short run, whatever the long term advantages to society, they are faced with all types of pressures from groups whose profits or employment are at stake. Moreover, the balance of imports and exports is a sensitive area for many governments, and any measure which may lead to higher imports is likely to be scrutinised closely. Unilateral tariff concessions are therefore difficult to sell domestically and a bilateral bargain is likely to be preferred in the majority of cases.

A GSP-type approach, then, can only go so far; moreover, it is probably inevitable that GSP schemes are surrounded with more or less strict safeguard clauses (also applied unilaterally and without warning or consultation) and restrictive rules of origin which would be unnecessary in a trading system based on most-favoured-nation access. Moreover, as some commentators have recently pointed out,[6] developing countries themselves could often, with advantage to their own allocative efficiency, reduce the levels of protection given in their own economies to inefficient, import-substituting industries. There is, therefore, some room for developing countries to take a more pragmatic approach to bargaining in the GATT negotiations than would result from a slavish adherence to pursuit of GSP concessions. As this chapter has indicated, the two GSP and the GATT negotiations are not mutually exclusive.

NOTES

1. A detailed analysis of ldcs' interests in the GATT negotiations can be found in Kathryn Morton, *A Hand Worth Playing*, ODI, 1974.
2. OECD, *Policy Prespectives for International Trade and Economic Relations.* Paris, 1972.
3. GATT Press Release 1134, 14 September 1973.
4. *Ibid*
5. See p. 20
6. e.g. B. Balassa in *The Structure of Protection in Developing Countries* (Johns Hopkins, 1971).

INDEX

For Product Safety Concerns and Information please contact our EU
representative GPSR@taylorandfrancis.com
Taylor & Francis Verlag GmbH, Kaufingerstraße 24, 80331 München, Germany

www.ingramcontent.com/pod-product-compliance
Ingram Content Group UK Ltd.
Pitfield, Milton Keynes, MK11 3LW, UK
UKHW021508240926
475702UK00035B/662
* 9 7 8 1 0 4 1 2 7 9 3 5 8 *